# Also By Brenda Hasse

<u>An Afterlife Journey Trilogy</u>

On The Third Day

From Beyond The Grave

Until We Meet Again

<u>Young Adult</u>

The Freelancer

A Lady's Destiny

The Moment Of Trust

Wilkinshire

<u>Picture Books For Children</u>

My Horsy And Me, What Can We Be?

Yes, I Am Loved

A Unicorn For My Birthday

# A Victim Of
# **Desperation**

~

# Brenda Hasse

A Victim Of Desperation

Copyright © 2021 by Brenda Hasse

All rights reserved. No part of the book may be used or reproduced by any means, graphic, electronic, or mechanical, including photocopying, recording, taping, or by any storage information retrieving system without the written permission of the publisher except in the case of brief quotations embodied in critical articles or reviews.

The characters in this novel are based on a true story of human trafficking. Their names have been changed. It is a work of fiction with some of the embellished details a work of the author's imagination.

Because of the dynamic nature of the Internet, and Web addresses or links may have changed since publication and may no longer be valid.

ISBN: 978-1-7347786-4-9 (pbk)

ISBN: 978-1-7347786-5-6 (ebk)

To S.K.

~

Many people are aware of human sex trafficking. However, human trafficking involves the following:

1. Sex trafficking
2. Forced labor, indentured servitude, and labor trafficking
3. Organ trafficking
4. Child soldier
5. Child marriage
6. Debt bondage

If you are aware of any human trafficking, please call or text the numbers below.

National Human Trafficking Hotline
1-888-373-7888 or text: 233733

# A Haunting Memory

I glanced at the radio on the dashboard for the time and exhaled as I scowled. A delay at work kept me longer than expected. Tightening my grip on the steering wheel, I imagined my daughter pacing in front of the dance studio even though I instructed her to wait safely inside the building until I arrived. After passing a car traveling well below the posted speed limit, I glanced at my speedometer, loosened my ten-and-two grip on the steering wheel, and eased my foot from the gas pedal. The last thing I needed today was a ticket.

My mind drifted to my to-do list: call the dentist for cleaning appointments for the five of us, try to reduce the pile of laundry that seems to magically double in size while I sleep at night, and stop at the grocery store to get the few items for dinner. I usually went to the grocery store before ten o'clock on Saturday mornings to avoid dodging carts and waiting for an indecisive individual to choose an item while standing in the center of an aisle. I cringed, assuming I would have to play bumper cars with my cart while gathering what I needed to make dinner. Was I being purposely delayed throughout my day for some mysterious reason?

    I was pulled from my thoughts as a sign on the side of the road caught my attention. Printed in black and white, I thought it was a political sign pleading for anyone's vote, but when I was close enough to read it, the gooseflesh on my arms began to prickle. The blood drained from my face, my heartbeat increased, and my palms became clammy as I read the few words printed on it. It offered an outrageous hourly pay for 'Summer Work,' 'Even With No Experience,' 'base-appt.' *Base appointment*? 'Text For Info" A phone number was printed at the bottom. I knew exactly the kind of sign this was. I exhaled, not realizing I had been holding my breath as I lifted my foot from the accelerator and pulled into the closest parking lot on the busy five-lane road lined with retail stores. Bringing my car to a stop, I stared at the two-sided sign and put my car in park.

## A VICTIM OF DESPERATION

The sign reminded me of an ad I answered in the newspaper nearly twenty years ago. Are these the same people? How can they still be in business? Haven't they been caught yet? Or maybe this is something even worse – sex trafficking. My imagination kicked into overdrive. How many people have seen this and sent an inquiring text? What if one of my daughters saw this sign and did so without me knowing?

I held my hands out before me. They were quivering, shaking uncontrollably as memories of a desperate decision I made long ago rose to the surface from the deep abyss where it had been buried within my mind.

# Meeting James

My mother owned and operated three businesses. My father played music in a band and was always on the road. Much of my childhood was spent in daycare. With each of my parents pursuing their dreams or perhaps avoiding their inability to get along, their marriage had little chance of surviving. They divorced just before my eleventh birthday.

Custody of my siblings and me was granted to my mother, and we resided with her during the week but saw her rarely since she owned three companies. Since my brother was a few years older than me, she allowed us to stay home under his supervision while she worked.

## A VICTIM OF DESPERATION

We were not always alone at home, though. Our housekeeper, Ramona, was there occasionally. When my brother went to live with Dad a few months after the divorce, I was left in charge.

According to the custody agreement, our weekends were spent with Dad. I knew when I got off the school bus on a Friday afternoon, he would be waiting in the driveway. He had a standing order for several take-out pizzas at the restaurant around the corner from his house, and we would pick them up for dinner on the way. He drove us home late Sunday afternoons. He was prompt, caring, and I knew I could always depend on him.

When I was sixteen, my kindhearted father took in a young man, Rob, who was five years older than me. Since he was from a broken home, Dad wanted to give him a chance in life and guide him toward living independently instead of ending up on welfare or, worse yet, on the streets. Rob was kind of quiet and settled into our divided family quickly.

One weekend, I carried the pizzas into the house and set them on the kitchen table. I turned to retrieve paper plates from the cupboard and saw Rob standing in the doorway leading into the living room. Someone standing behind him, peeking over Rob's shoulder, transfixed, staring at me. I stood dumbfounded, unexpecting a guest.

Rob motioned over his shoulder with a fisted hand and thumb extended. "Jess, this is James. He goes by Jim." He stepped into the room and motioned toward me to complete the introduction. "Jim, Jess." Walking past me, Rob went to the table and began opening the boxes of pizza.

My first impression, Jim was older, much older than I was, maybe by ten years. His eyes were the color of a blue sky on a cloudless day. He was quite tall, with curly brunette hair framing his face. He nodded at me, displaying a slight smile.

"Hi, Jess."

"Hello." The sound of his voice was enough to snap me out of my trance. I retrieved the paper plates, napkins, and forks, adding one of each, assuming Jim was joining us for dinner.

Dad brought an extra chair from the dining while I set the table. Our family sat in our usual unassigned places, bowed our heads, and said grace. I peeked from beneath my eyebrows and glanced around the table. Everyone's head was bowed toward their plates except for one. Jim was looking at me. I looked down at my empty plate.

## A VICTIM OF DESPERATION

I glanced toward Jim several times throughout the meal, always catching him staring at me. He would divert his eyes like a disobedient child caught doing something he should not be doing. Why did he keep looking at me? I brushed my napkin across my face in case there was a crumb of food dangling from the corner of my mouth. Was I flattered or uncomfortable under his watchful eyes? The situation was confusing.

Jim became a regular at my Dad's house. He made a point to include me in conversations and join him and Rob when they went out for a late-night snack at a drive-thru or to a movie. He was attentive, polite, and opened doors for me to enter before him. I was flattered. He made me feel important, special, and appreciated.

My imagination entertained the idea of dating Jim. I was only sixteen, much too young for him to be interested in me. Was it curiosity I was feeling, a crush, or something more? It did not take long for me to find out.

"Hey, let's go get some ice cream." Jim sat forward, leaning his forearms on the top of his thighs as the three of us sat in the living room watching a movie.

I looked at Jim and Rob sitting on the couch. "Sounds good. I could go for some ice cream." I collapsed the footrest on the recliner and stood.

Rob placed his hand on his stomach. "Not me. My stomach is a little queasy from dinner. Too many pepper seeds on my pizza, I think. I'll pass." He sighed before returning his attention to the movie.

Jim stood. "Then, I guess it's just us, Jess."

I looked at Rob. "Do you want us to bring something back for you?"

"No, thanks."

Dad looked up from his newspaper he was reading at the kitchen table as we walked to the backdoor. "Where are you two going?" He turned a page as he waited for a reply.

I paused with my hand on the doorknob. "Out for ice cream. Do you want any?"

He remained unsmiling as he glanced at Jim with a wary glare. "Here, let me give you some money." He reached into his back pocket for his wallet.

"No, I got it." Jim patted the pocket of his jeans.

Dad opened his wallet and handed me three dollars. "Thanks, Jim, but she can pay for her ice cream."

I fanned out the dollar bills in my hand. Dad had given me just enough to cover the cost of what I would get, nothing more. "Thanks, Dad."

Jim opened his car door for me to get into the passenger seat. I buckled my seatbelt as he sat and put the key in the ignition. He glanced at me before putting the car into reverse. "I don't think your dad likes me very much."

I scowled as I looked at him. "Why would you say that?"

"Just an impression I get from him."

The ice cream shop was a short distance away. We arrived close to closing time, ordered quickly, sat on a nearby picnic table to eat our sundaes.

Jim spooned ice cream into his mouth before pointing his plastic spoon toward me. "You know, I like you. You are easy to talk to and, if I may say so myself, quite pretty." Jim leaned forward to eat a dripping spoonful of hot fudge but was not quick enough. "Damn." A glob splatted onto his thigh. "Get me a napkin." He ordered.

Leaving my sundae on the table, I hurried to the counter where we placed our order and pulled several napkins from the dispenser. I handed them to Jim before returning to my seat.

He wiped the mess from his pant leg. "I think you and I should go out."

I chuckled. "We are out."

"No, I mean date, like a couple."

My heart did a summersault in my chest. *Date*? I had never dated anyone before. How should I act? What should I say? This was all new to me. Only one word popped into my mind. "Sure." Then it dawned on me that I would only see him on weekends. "But I am gone all week, so how is 'dating' supposed to work."

"We can talk on the phone during the week and see each other on weekends when you are at your Dad's house." He shoved his empty plastic bowl and napkin across the table toward me.

I finished the last few bites of my sundae and threw our containers in the trashcan.

We drove back to the house and pulled into the driveway. Jim put the car in park.

"I need to get home." He leaned toward me, placed his index finger beneath my chin to lift it upward, and placed a gentle kiss upon my lips. As his mouth hovered over mine when he finished, he stared into my eyes. "Goodnight, Jess. Sweet dreams."

"Goodnight." I got out of the car, unable to keep the smile off my face as my stomach fluttered like a butterfly was inside it, and my footsteps defied gravity, a summer romance. I drifted off to sleep that night, dreaming of my first boyfriend.

~

Dating an older guy had its demands, or should I say, required me to meet his needs. Unfortunately, just

## A VICTIM OF DESPERATION

before my seventeenth birthday, a week before Thanksgiving, a pregnancy test confirmed I was pregnant. Jim was not happy, but he also was not upset. In fact, he did not seem to care. I was scared. What would my parents think? Mom took the news in stride.

I decided it would be best to break the news to Dad in person. I took a deep breath as I saw him waiting in the driveway on Friday after school. Once we arrived at his house, I set the pizzas on the kitchen table.

"Dad, can I talk to you for a second." I watched as he nodded his head before following me into the living room. I sat on the sofa and took a deep breath as he stood before me.

"I'm pregnant."

"Jim's baby?"

I watched as the vein in his forehead enlarged and began to pulse. He knew my pregnancy had occurred during his watch, so to speak. I was aware of his dislike for Jim. His disdain had only deepened since learning of my condition.

"Jess, you have to get an abortion." Dad pleaded as he paced the living room floor.

"I'm nearly three months. The baby has a heartbeat. I'm not going to kill it."

He stopped pacing and cupped both hands over his mouth to calm himself. He looked at me as he lowered his hands. "Jess, this will change your life forever, maybe even ruin it."

I knew he had my best interest at heart, but I knew I would be able to go through with the pregnancy, and Jim would be there to help raise the baby. "I'll manage."

"How? You aren't out of high school. You don't have a job. How are you going to provide for a baby?"

"Jim and I will work it out."

Dad put his fisted hands on his hips. "Speaking of Jim, why isn't he here breaking the news to me?"

"He thought it would be better if I did so by myself."

"Of course, he did." He ran his hand through his graying auburn hair pulling it back over his head. "Even though I don't agree with your decision, I'll support it and help you any way I can."

Tears welled in my eyes. I was scared. What he said was true. My life would never be the same. I went to him, put my arms around his abdomen, and squeezed slightly. "Thanks, Dad."

# Ashamed

Murmured conversations echoed off the walls as I passed other students in the hallway while heading to my next class. I tried to ignore their inquisitive stares at my abdomen and tilted heads deep in whispered gossip. During my third hour class, I was summoned to the office and escorted to the principal, where my mother sat in a chair before his desk. My counselor stood by the open door and motioned toward the empty chair, indicating I should sit. She closed the door and took her place behind the principal's desk with her arms crossed over her chest as she leaned against the wall with a grim expression on her face.

The principal sat erect in his high-back leather chair with his fingers woven together, his hands resting on the edge of his desk blotter, and a manila file open before him.

"So, Jessica, you are expecting a baby. Do you know your due date?"

"In June."

"Well," he smiled slightly, "we have a strict policy about teenage pregnancy in our district. We generously provide funding for an expectant mother to attend a private school."

I glanced at my mother before looking back to the principal. "A private school?"

"Yes, you see, we have had several parents who have become aware of your condition and insist we follow school policy. They are afraid their daughters may make the same choice that you have. As you can see, this puts me in an awkward position. I have verified with the superintendent, and he agrees we must follow the policy for everyone's sake. So, you will attend a private school beginning the second semester, at our expense, of course. I have sent the necessary transfer papers to the principal at your new school. She is making the arrangements for your admission and will call you to set up an appointment to discuss your classes and set goals for the second semester. With any luck, you should be able to complete your junior year before the baby arrives."

My stomach tightened as if he had thrown a punch at it. My cheeks seemed warm, very warm. Was I embarrassed or angry? Maybe both. I was being ordered to leave my friends and attend a school where I knew no one? Was I banished from school because I was pregnant?

The principal looked at my mother. "Is there a particular day and time you can meet with the private school principal? It would be wise for the two of you to see her before Christmas break. Exams are scheduled once we return, and we don't want to interrupt your daughter's exam schedule."

I did not hear my mother's reply. The principal picked up the receiver of his phone and made a phone call. My nightmare unfolded before my eyes as I sat and watched numbly, unable to react.

The counselor gathered the loose papers and picked up the file from the principal's desk. She stuffed it into a large interoffice envelope and handed it to my mother. "Everything is in here."

"Thank you." My mother accepted the envelope, stood, and shook hands with the counselor, who released her hand and opened the office door.

The principal scribbled something on a small piece of pink paper, hung up the phone, and handed the memo to my mom as he stood.

"Thank you." She shook his hand and followed me out of the room.

Once outside the office, I began walking down the hallway to return to class.

"Where are you going?" Mom was staring at me as I turned around.

"Back to class."

"Our appointment with the other principal is now."

My mouth dropped open. "Now? What about my books I left in the classroom?"

"Go and get them. I'll meet you in the car out front."

My mind raced as I walked back to class. Things were happening so quickly.

As I entered the classroom, everyone redirected their attention from the teacher speaking at the podium and looked at me. I gathered my books and backpack and shut the door as quietly as the hydraulic closer at the top of the solid wooden door would allow. A quick stop at the bathroom was necessary before meeting mom at the car.

## A VICTIM OF DESPERATION

"Am I being excused from the rest of my classes for the day?" I sighed as I sat in the passenger seat and slammed the door shut.

"I will call the school and make sure you are." She released the brake and drove out of the circular driveway.

The private school was only a few miles away. Strange, I was unaware it existed. As we pulled into the driveway and parked the car in front of the entrance, I stared at the enormous, ancient building that resembled an asylum. "Impressive." The brick exterior was clean, neat, and well maintained. I got out of the car and scanned the breathtaking Victorian architecture.

The door to the school opened. A woman stood in the doorway and waved. "Hello, I presume you are Jessica and Jessica's mom?" She displayed a genuine smile.

As apprehensive as I was, her infectious smile caused me to grin and feel at ease. "Yes." I climbed the handful of steps of the entrance.

"We are excited to have you with us. Welcome." She motioned with her hand for us to proceed through the door as she held it open.

The interior of the school complimented the exterior architecture with its dark wooden wainscoting along the hallway. I looked up at the ceiling to see domed school light fixtures dotted down the center of the long corridor. A beige tile with a chocolate border, a foot from the wall's edge, covered the floor.

"As you can see, our building is quite old but well maintained. We appreciate its character and history." The principal explained as we walked down the hallway and were ushered into her office. "I'm Mrs. Dennis, the principal."

Mom handed her my file, and we sat in the two chairs in front of the large oak desk.

Mrs. Dennis opened the file as she sat, put on a pair of reading glasses, and examined the paperwork. She looked at me. "So, you are expecting a baby. Congratulations." Her smile was kind.

I was uncertain if she stated a compliment or was being sarcastic? I thought it best to be polite. "Thank you."

"I see you are a junior and should easily be able to complete your second semester while in attendance with us."

I had given some thought to the remainder of this school year. My due date was close to the end of the second semester. I had passed every class thus far and had only a few more credits to complete before being classified as a senior. Unsure of how I would manage school and a baby, I entertained an aggressive idea. I sat a little taller in my chair as I proposed the tough question. "Mrs. Dennis, is it possible for me to complete my junior and senior classes and graduate from high school in June?"

In my peripheral vision, I saw my mom turn her head toward me. She was surprised by my question.

The principal looked over the rim of her glasses momentarily, thumbed through the papers in my file, and counted the credits I had earned to date. Her eyebrows raised, and she nodded her head approvingly. "I see you are currently taking a full load of classes now. You have an impressive grade point average. Are you receiving a passing grade in all of your current classes?"

"Yes."

"I will have to speak to a counselor to verify." She glanced down at my file and nodded in confirmation. "From what I can see, once you have completed your junior first semester, there is a possibility you will be able to take enough credits while attending classes during the day, independent studies, and night classes to graduate in June. It would be a heavy class load, but it can be done."

I sighed and nodded with a smile. "Good. I would like to graduate before having my baby."

Mrs. Dennis removed her glasses and rose from her desk. "Then let's have you meet with a counselor to schedule your classes. Come with me."

She led us down a narrow hallway, stopped before an office, and knocked on the door before motioning to the empty chairs outside of the room. "Have a seat. I'll be just a moment while I review your file with Mrs. Norton." She entered the office and shut the door.

I sat and looked up and down the empty hallway.

Mom sighed. "Jess, are you sure you want to take on so many classes?"

"Mom, I don't see how I am going to go to school and take care of a baby, too? I'd just as soon get my high school education behind me."

The door opened, and Mrs. Dennis stepped into the hallway. "Mrs. Norton is ready to see you. Jessica, we are glad you are here. If you have any questions or issues, please feel free to come and see me anytime."

"Thank you, Mrs. Dennis."

Mom and I entered the tiny office and sat in the chairs before Mrs. Norton's desk.

"Hello. I'm Mrs. Norton, and I will be your counselor. Jessica, I understand you want an aggressive schedule to accommodate your graduation from high school in June. Is that correct?"

"Yes."

"Very well."

Over the next hour or so, we established what credits I needed, outlining my schedule, independent studies, and evening classes.

"I think you are all set. Once you finish your exams at your present school, you will begin classes here the following week."

"Is there any possibility I may begin my independent study classes over Christmas break?"

Her eyebrows raised, and she smiled. "That is an excellent idea. Let me get the material together for you, and I will call when it is ready for you to pick up."

"Thank you."

# Doing My Best

My Christmas break involved finishing two independent study classes, spending the weekends at Dad's house, and celebrating the holiday with my family and Jim. After taking my semester exams and achieving grades that exceeded my expectation, I transferred to the private school the following week. I began pushing myself under the heavy class load toward graduation.

At seventeen-years-old, I graduated from high school with a 3.8-grade point average and proudly attended, big belly and all, my high school graduation ceremony in June. Two days later, I gave birth to a baby girl.

## A VICTIM OF DESPERATION

I held my daughter in my arms, admiring her perfect little face. I counted her ten little fingers and ten little toes and named her Heather. I thought of the relationship I had with my mother or lack thereof.

"I promise you, baby Heather, to be a better mother to you than my mother is to me. I will protect you, be supportive, and always be by your side, even when you don't want me there. Above all, I will make sure you know that I love you."

I looked at the doorway as Dad walked into my hospital room, carrying a vase of flowers and a pink metallic helium balloon.

"There is the little one." His voice was a mere whisper as he set my gifts on the nightstand, leaned toward my forehead, and kissed it.

"Grandpa, this is Heather, your granddaughter." I placed my newborn baby in his awaiting arms.

"Hello, sweetheart." He gingerly sat in the cushioned chair near my bed and traced his finger along the side of her cheek. "My, you are a beautiful little one, just like your mama."

Heather wrapped her tiny hand around his index finger, securing her place within his heart. I watched as he smiled, mirroring the growing affection in his eyes. He looked at me as I turned and sat cross-legged in bed, facing him.

"You, Jim, and Heather are a family now, in a way," he began sarcastically, "so, I have prepared a bedroom for the three of you to share at my house."

I looked down at my entwined fingers in my lap. "I know you don't like Jim, so we had planned to get an apartment."

"I didn't say I did not like him. Honestly, I don't trust him, and I am afraid he will mistreat you and the baby badly."

I looked at Dad, puzzled by his train of thought. "Trust him? Mistreat me badly? You make him sound like a monster."

"Let's just say I have taken notice of certain characteristics and behavior that you have failed to see. If you live under my roof, I can ensure you and this little one will remain safe. I have talked it over with your mother, and she likes the idea too, so you will be living with me full-time."

*Safe*? Was Dad worried Jim would hurt the baby or me?

"Don't worry, old man. I can take care of her and my daughter too." Jim entered my hospital room, staring at my dad, challenging him. His line of vision shifted to my face. "Right, Jess?"

I was too emotionally drained from giving birth to argue with either of them. Dad's comments lingered in my mind, forming apprehension and doubt. Jim was a decade older than me. Why was he still living with his parents and only worked part-time in construction? How would he afford an apartment for the three of us?

Dad rose and placed Heather in my arms, his face flushed with anger as he looked at Jim. "Technically, Jess is not your wife. She is a minor, and she will remain under my roof until I say so. Or do I have to get the court involved?"

"Jess?" Jim's eyes narrowed as he awaited my answer.

I looked at Dad, reading his body language. He was serious. I shrugged my shoulders. "Dad is right. I am only seventeen, and I want to attend college in the fall." My boyfriend glared at me as I went on to explain, "Jim, he means what he says. He will take you to court. We can stay with him until I can get a job, help with our expenses, and save some money for an apartment."

Dad sighed. "Then it's settled." He kissed my cheek. "If you attend night classes, I can watch the baby." He stroked Heather's cheek with his index finger before storming past Jim on his way out of the room. What followed was a heated argument between Jim and me. Jim lost.

After I was released from the hospital, the three of us moved into the room Dad had prepared for us. I became acutely aware of the suspicious tone in his voice and watchful eyes from behind a newspaper. He did not have to say what his body language revealed; he secretly wanted my boyfriend to move out of the house.

I was determined to attend college in the autumn and earn a college degree. Once completed, I could qualify for a good-paying job. My accomplishment would set a good example for Heather too. Unfortunately, I did not have a vehicle to go to and from campus and could not afford to buy one. My luck changed when my older brother told me he was getting rid of his van and purchasing a new one. Words could not describe how thankful I was when he handed me the keys to his old van. I was the proud owner of a 1994 Dodge Caravan with faux wood-paneled sides. It was in rough shape, and the back seats were missing because he had used the space to transport his tools and other equipment for his construction job.

Now that I had transportation, I enrolled at the community college. To pay for my classes, gas, groceries, and other expenses, I babysat two children before and after they rode the bus to school three days a week. On the days I did not babysit, I attended late afternoon and evening classes and worked at McDonald's until closing. Jim continued his part-time job in plastering and drywalling. Dad watched Heather when needed. It was a blessing to not have to pay for daycare.

The demands of motherhood, girlfriend, student, and my two jobs was a lot to handle. Heather had yet to sleep through the night. When she napped during the day, I studied. When Jim came home late afternoons, he wanted my undivided attention and barked orders. "Get me a beer." "Make me a sandwich." "What's for dinner?" "We are eating what? If you love me, you will make me something else." He never apologized for his mistakes, lack of manners, or unkind words.

With two more mouths to feed in the household, Dad's grocery bill increased, yet Jim did not offer to pay his share. I guess he thought the contribution I made to the fund was his portion as well. To add insult to injury, his father often sent him money in the mail, which he spent on himself.

Two weeks after my eighteenth birthday and the completion of my first semester of college, I had enough of being Jim's enabler. The vail of love was pulled away from my eyes to reveal what Dad saw in my boyfriend, a lazy, arrogant, manipulative, controlling loser. When we first moved into Dad's house, I thought it would be good for the three of us to remain a family unit, to make our relationship work, but Heather deserved a better father, and I deserved someone better than Jim.

With our fragile relationship in splinters, he packed his belongings and paused in the doorway before he left. "Heather is my daughter. I will fight you for custody and never pay you a dime of child support."

The door slammed shut. I turned to Dad. "Can he do that?"

"I will contact my attorney and have you file for custody tomorrow."

To put some distance between myself and Jim, I moved back to Mom's house but knew I could not stay there forever.

# Let The Battle Begin

I decided to cast aside my dream of earning a college degree. Even though Heather and I were living temporarily with Mom, I needed to provide for my daughter and find a place of our own. The sooner, the better. My Aunt Sarah owned a tanning salon and offered me a job, which I accepted. Jim adamantly refused to accept his financial responsibility for our daughter. I imagined he would continue to do so until his hand was forced, and even then, he would ignore any requirements set forth by the court.

Dad and I met with his attorney before my custody hearing. He explained my case was simple. I would retain full custody of Heather and receive child support. Jim would be granted visitation rights, but they would be kept to a minimum.

On the morning of the hearing, I arranged for my Aunt Angela, who had a daycare in her home, to watch Heather. I dropped her off on the way to the courthouse. Dressed conservatively, I met Dad in the lobby. I was confident the law was on my side, but that did not stop my hands and insides from trembling. I took a deep breath, lifted my chin, and walked down the hallway with Dad by my side. My attorney met us at the security scanner with his briefcase in hand.

We waited in line to go through the checkpoint, which gave me a moment to look around at the white walls decorated with court themed pictures. The building was more modern than I expected. I thought it would be like the architecture in the private school I attended. It was more like a sterile hospital.

Once through security, my attorney escorted us into the courtroom. We sat in the chairs behind a short railing to wait for our case to be called. I listened as the judge spoke. He seemed nice, his comments fair, even though his bushy eyebrows projected a rather mean and intimidating persona. His bench resembled the faux woodgrain of my van. The railing looked like a row of

## A VICTIM OF DESPERATION

large match sticks, the floor was tile, and my cushionless seat was made of wood.

Jim entered the room. He was alone and sat in the seats on the opposite side of the aisle. I avoided making eye contact with him.

As our case was called, my attorney ushered us to a table where we sat before the judge. Jim sat behind the empty table opposite us.

The bailiff accepted a file from my lawyer and gave it to the judge, who opened it and scanned several papers. He looked over his reading glasses at me and then to Jim.

"Sir, you do not have an attorney present?"

"No." Jim remained seated. I thought he should have stood and replied, 'no, sir.'

"Would you like me to appoint counsel to assist you?" The judge inquired.

"No, I got it."

The judge raised his eyebrows in doubt before looking at me. "Well, Jessica, I see you are asking for full custody and child support."

I stood. "Yes, Sir."

"Please, be seated." He waited for me to do so. "How old were you when you became pregnant?"

I blinked my eyes, taken back by his question. "I was sixteen."

The judge's eyebrows drew together, making a unibrow. He stared at Jim. "How old were you when she became pregnant?"

"Twenty-five." He shrugged his shoulder.

"And you are the child's father?"

My dad shifted in his chair.

"Yes." Jim pursed his lips as if proud.

"Jessica, did you consent to have intercourse with this man?"

"Yes." I wanted to explain more about our relationship but had been advised by my attorney to answer his questions directly, with no elaboration.

The judge narrowed his eyes and glared at Jim. "At age twenty-five, having sex, consensual or otherwise, with anyone under the age of eighteen is classified as statutory rape." He looked at me. "I see you have omitted the charge from your lawsuit."

My lawyer rose from his chair. "Your honor, my client has opted not to file charges since she consented to have intercourse."

The judge glanced from me to Jim and back again. "Very well." He leaned toward a woman sitting at a desk next to him. She scribbled something on a piece of paper, stapled a business card to the top, and hand it to the judge.

## A VICTIM OF DESPERATION

The judge examined the paper to ensure all was in order. "Jim, you are allowed to have custody of your daughter every other weekend and must pay $281 a month in child support." He handed the paper to the bailiff, who gave it to my lawyer. He banged the gavel on a wooden disk. "Case dismissed."

Jim stormed out of the room.

My lawyer turned to me as I stood. "Let's talk in the hallway."

We found a vacant bench in a quiet corridor. Dad and I sat.

I looked up at my attorney. "He only has to pay me $281 a month? That isn't very much."

"I know. The woman calculated his payment based on the yearly income he submitted to the court. He reported a low amount."

I shook my head in disbelief, frustration, or perhaps both.

My attorney continued. "He may receive most of his salary in cash, so it is not reported."

"That doesn't help me any." I rolled my lips inward as I wondered how I would provide for Heather on my own.

My lawyer sighed and gave me the paper the woman had filled out. He pointed to the attached business card. "That is the name of a person who can help you collect unpaid child support or when you have other issues. He is known as the Friend of the Court. Call him and make an appointment."

"So, if Jim doesn't pay his child support, I am to call him?"

"Yes."

"OK. Thank you for all that you have done."

My dad stood and shook the lawyer's hand. "Thank you. Send the bill to me."

"You are welcome." He turned to me and shook my hand. "Good luck. I have a feeling you are going to do just fine."

"Thanks. I hope so." I watched my attorney walk away, too stunned to follow. I looked at Dad and sighed, exhaling my pent-up tension. "Well, what do you think?"

"I think you have a fight on your hands. It won't be easy, you may receive a few battle scars, but you will survive."

~

Eager to establish a good relationship with the Friend of the Court, I called the phone number on the card the next morning and made an appointment for the following week to meet Mr. West.

## A VICTIM OF DESPERATION

During our meeting, he explained his responsibilities, how I would receive my child support, and encouraged me to contact him with any issues Jim and I could not solve. I had a feeling I would be talking to Mr. West quite often.

## My Independence

Over the next three months, I scrimped and saved for a security deposit and the first month's rent for an apartment. A refund from my tax return increased the balance of my savings account substantially, and I vowed to leave it untouched unless I exhausted all other means of attaining needed cash.

On the first of April, I signed a lease for an apartment. My first apartment! I packed and accumulated hand-me-downs from Mom. Her boyfriend, more like my second dad, helped me move my things while Mom kept Heather occupied in her new bedroom.

## A VICTIM OF DESPERATION

We enjoyed a take-out lunch together before assembling the crib.

"Thanks for all of your help." I carried Heather on my hip and walked Mom and her boyfriend to the door.

"Well, now the fun part begins – unpacking." Mom and her boyfriend hugged me and kissed Heather's cheek. I waved good-bye before closing the door, turning to stare at the boxes and disheveled furniture, and smiled.

I put Heather down for a nap, opened a box labeled 'kitchen,' and began stocking the cupboards with mom's old wedding dishes and silverware. Why she kept them, I will never know, but I was glad she did. I assembled my bed and arranged the living room furniture. With most of the work done for the day, I sat on the sofa, tired but satisfied. I was finally on my own in a small apartment. It had two bedrooms and one bathroom. Drapes were not included, so I hung the spare set of sheets over the windows with push pins.

I continued to work part-time at the tanning salon and acquired two additional jobs. I babysat two little girls when I was not working at the salon and moonlighted at a Coney restaurant. It was challenging to juggle all three jobs and spend time with Heather, but I did what I needed to do to provide for us.

I especially liked the sales position at the tanning salon. I had to sign up customers for memberships, clean and sterilize the tanning beds, and sell products. I received a commission of ten percent per sale. The frequent and loyal customers usually purchase better tanning lotions, adding more money to my paycheck. A stunningly beautiful woman named Candy always bought lotions from me. I estimated her age was between 28 to 30 years old, tall, an androgynous-looking woman with short blonde hair and baby blue eyes. She told me she was an exotic dancer and liked to keep her body a lovely bronze.

"It looks better under the lights." She admitted.

Jim demanded his visitation rights and took Heather once a week. He soon increased his visitation to an entire weekend and would skip his scheduled time with her if he had something else planned. He had yet to pay child support, and my calls to Mr. West seemed to fall on deaf ears with no results.

After filling my van with gas and buying groceries and other necessities from the dollar store, I kept a minimal amount of cash in my purse, just enough to get by, and added the remainder of my weekly pay to my savings account. My aunt watched Heather when I was at work, and I gladly paid her for her time. It was comforting to know she was in good hands and safe.

## A VICTIM OF DESPERATION

Finding myself on a Sunday morning not scheduled to work, I decided to visit Mom for two reasons. One, to do my laundry for free. Two, so she could play with Heather.

I drove down her street and spotted someone familiar exiting his car in the driveway across the way from Mom's house. I stopped my van and rolled down the window.

"Hey, stranger! I have not seen you in a long time." It was Danny. His grandma lived across the street from Mom. When I was younger, his family visited her every Sunday for brunch after church, and we often played together in the afternoon. He was a few years older than me, but we got along just fine. I watched as he approached my van.

"Hi." He smiled before glancing at my mom's house. "Do you still live with your mom?"

"No, I live in an apartment. I am stopping by for a visit and to do my laundry."

"Nice."

"Give me a call sometime, and we'll have to get caught up."

"I will. Talk to you soon."

Mom met us at the door and presented Heather with a new toy as I carried my dirty clothes to the laundry room and started a load. The three of us visited and ate lunch together while the last load of my laundry dried. Mom buckled Heather in her car seat while I put my clean clothes in the van. I kept Heather awake during the ride home and laid her down in her bed for her nap while I put clothes away.

~

After a busy week at the tanning salon and watching the girls, I was thankful to have the night off from the restaurant, which did not usually happen on a Friday night. I was ready to crawl in bed after putting Heather down for the night after finishing the dishes when my phone rang. I grabbed the receiver from the wall as I placed the dried plate in the cupboard. "Hello."

"Hi, Jess." It was Danny.

I hesitated before replying. "How did you get my phone number."

"From your mom." He admitted.

Partway through our conversation about old times together, I put Heather to bed while Danny waited on the phone for me to return. When he heard me yawn, he suggested we get together on a Sunday and insisted on bringing dinner. I checked my calendar to ensure I had the night off at the restaurant and agreed.

## A VICTIM OF DESPERATION

Two days later, I answered a knock on my door to see him holding a bucket of chicken and a tray of drinks. "Hi." I smiled.

"Hey, I thought your address sounded familiar. My cousin, Kathy, lives in an apartment next door to you. Weird, huh?" He nodded his head toward the door down the hall.

"Really?"

"Let me see if she is home, and I'll introduce you." He handed me the chicken before knocking on her door.

Heather dashed for the open door as she crawled with the speed of a cheetah into the hallway. I set the food on the floor, picked her up, and placed her on my hip. I watched as the apartment door next to mine opened.

"Danny! This is an unexpected visit."

"I know. I want you to meet Jess. She just moved in next door to you." He took a step back to allow Kathy to step into the hallway, which was soon followed by two little girls peeking out the doorway at me.

Danny made the introductions. "Jess, this is Kathy and her minions. Kathy, this is Jess and Heather."

I wondered how Danny had known my daughter's name but guessed Mom had told him.

"It's nice to meet you, Jess and Heather." Kathy greeted.

"Same here." I smiled. Her hazel eyes sparkled, and her smile was genuine. Her auburn hair was pulled back in a thick ponytail.

"If you need anything, feel free to ask. I'm a single mom, and I stay home full-time."

"Thanks. I work a lot, but I will keep you in mind if I have an emergency or run out of sugar or something. It's nice to meet you."

Kathy became a trustworthy neighbor and friend. We took turns watching each other's children whenever needed. It was comforting to have someone I could depend on. Danny continued to visit, our relationship strengthened, and we began dating.

I hosted a small party to celebrate Heather's first birthday in June. Even though I invited Jim, he did not attend. He gave the lame excuse of hosting a birthday celebration for her at his parent's house. In truth, I believe he was avoiding Dad's lecture on his failure to pay child support and being a deadbeat dad.

Once his lease expired, Danny moved into my apartment a month later. He worked in construction during the day and agreed to split the rent, utilities, and groceries to ease my burdens. It was nice to have a boyfriend who paid his fair share. He was glad to watch

## A VICTIM OF DESPERATION

Heather when I work on weekends and nights. My aunt continued to watch her weekdays.

As the summer days were crossed off my wall calendar, my savings slowly dwindled. I barely earned enough to pay half of my rent, the upkeep and gas for my van, and food. I was able to contribute to our telephone expense. I could not afford the luxury of a cellphone.

I sat at the kitchen table and stared at the pile of bills before me. The balance in my checking account was near negative. I emptied my mason jar of tip change onto the table and began counting. Its total and my weekly income were enough to get me by for another week or two. Vowing to leave the money in my savings account untouched, I could not fathom my ability or luck to come up with the money for the remainder of this month's expenses. Working at a Coney at night was mostly a waste of my time, except for Wednesdays when it was all you can eat fish and chips. The tips were meager, and the hourly pay a complete joke. I knew I had to do something. Work four jobs and never sleep? I had to come up with another source of income. I could sell what I had of value. Unfortunately, the only thing I had of value was my van, and I could not do without it. Perhaps it was my pride, but I wanted to do this on my own, to prove my capability to my parents, myself, and most of all, Jim.

I reported to the restaurant after Danny arrived home. Time ticked by. I waited on the only two customers I had in the past three hours. I picked up today's newspaper from the counter and tossed it in the garbage before lifting the empty coffee mug and washing away the coffee ring. I set the cup in the dirty dish bin for the dishwasher, turned, and looked at the newspaper as an idea came to mind. I retrieved the disheveled, folded newspaper. Was it possible a job was posted in the want ads I could do for extra money? Maybe a job which paid more than what I earned at the Coney or one where I could work from home like assemble something in the evenings and on weekends. After ensuring my customers' coffee cups were topped off, I placed the newspaper on a table in a vacant booth, sat, and paged through it until I found the classified ads. My finger traced down the column of available jobs. Welding, mechanic, truck driver. I exhaled as hopelessness settled within my chest. My finger stopped on an ad in the bottom left corner of the page. 'Make $500 A Week,' 'No experience needed,' 'Call today for an interview.' A local phone number was listed. I leaned back against the booth. *How much?* I leaned forward and reread the ad. It failed to state what the job entailed or anything about the hours. Was it full-time? Part-time? It was late in the evening. Dare I try to call at this hour? They were probably closed, but if no one answered the phone, I could leave a message. I went to the kitchen, picked up the phone receiver hanging on the wall, and dialed. After two rings, a man answered.

"Hello, this is Josh of …."

He rattled off something quickly. I could not understand what he said.

"Hello, I'm calling about the ad in the paper."

"And you are?"

"Jessica."

"Hello, Jessica. I can schedule an interview for you on Monday. Does 3:00 work for you?"

"If you don't mind me asking, what is the job?"

He paused for a moment. "Sales."

Sales? My mind raced. I am outgoing, a people person. Working at the Coney and tanning salon, both sales, technically? 3:00? I was still babysitting the girls at that time. Danny could be home by 4:00 if I ask him, but then again, his boss may not allow him to leave. I could ask Kathy to watch the children until he arrived home. A later appointment would be better, so I would not have to impose too much on her time.

"I am busy until 4:00. How about 4:30?"

"Fine, I will pencil you in." He gave me the office address. "Dress your best, bring a resume, and I'll see you then."

"Sure thing. Thank you."

What had just happened? I had an interview for a job that I could make a lot of money. I smiled. I could be making $500 a week. I could quit babysitting, walk away from the tanning salon and the Coney. I could save for a new car and a cell phone, so I could call to check on Heather when working.

When I got home from my shift, I plopped down on the couch next to Danny, who was drinking a beer while watching TV.

"I applied for a job tonight and have an interview on Monday. I can make $500 a week." I could hardly contain myself as I smiled from ear to ear.

Ignoring me, he stared at the program he was watching, seemingly unimpressed by my news. Was he jealous of the possibility that I could earn more per week than he did? He simply nodded before taking a sip from his beer—stupid male ego. I tried to state it another way.

"Just think, I may be able to quit babysitting. No more coming home to a bunch of children running around the apartment and making messes. I can even quit working at the restaurant and the tanning salon."

He just nodded once.

## A VICTIM OF DESPERATION

I stood and jammed my fisted hands on my hips as I stood, glaring at him. "Well, don't get too excited."

"We'll see if you get the job first." He raised his beer to take another swig but paused with it midway to his mouth. "What company? What will you be doing?"

"Sales. I don't remember the company name." I lied.

~

I woke the next morning, made a cup of coffee, and contemplated a way to compose a resume. Before the girls arrived, I put Heather on my hip, went to Kathy's apartment, and knocked on her door.

"Hey, what's up?" She greeted. Her two curious children peeked around the side of her legs before stepping in front of her.

"I need to go to the library and type up a resume. I have an interview on Monday. It shouldn't be very long. I hate to ask you, but can you watch the kids for an hour or so?"

"Sure. Wow! A job interview. You'll have to tell me all about it once you get back from the library."

"I will. So, give me about a half-hour to get ready before you come over."

"OK."

"Thanks." I prepared breakfast for Heather and the girls, who would arrive soon. Heather held her arms up, eager to eat. With her securely situated in her highchair, I went to the bathroom, quickly applied mascara and a little blush before there was a knock on the door, and I heard it open.

"Hey, Jess, the girls are here." The mom removed her daughter's jackets and hung them in the closet. Heather squeal as she greeted her two friends.

"OK, I'll be right out. Breakfast is on the kitchen table." I could hear the girls chattering as they eagerly went to the kitchen table.

"They are all set. Have a good day."

"I will, thanks." I heard the door close as I stuffed my makeup case in the cupboard under the bathroom sink. The girls were shoveling cereal into their mouths while Heather tried to stand in her highchair, indicating she was done. I quickly wet the end of a dishtowel, cleaned her hands and face, and set her in front of a pile of toys on the floor to play. I got a pad of paper and pen from the end table drawer and joined the girls at the table. "Is your cereal good?"

The oldest shoved a spoonful into her mouth. "It's my favorite."

"That's nice, but don't talk with your mouth full. It's impolite." I jotted down my skills and job experience

## A VICTIM OF DESPERATION

to include in my resume hoping to type it up quickly once I arrived at the library.

I had just added the last bit of information when Kathy knocked before entering with her girls in tow. I looked up at her as I set my pen on the table.

"I'll be as quick as possible." I rose and pulled my sweater from the closet.

"Take your time. The girls will enjoy playing with each other."

"Thanks, Kathy." I hurried to my van, started it, and glanced at the gas gauge—less than an eighth of a tank. The library was close enough to walk to, but time was of the essence.

I paused in the doorway to watch the beehive of activity within its rows of books. It was busy for a Saturday. Children were busy selecting books, several adults were sitting in cozy chairs reading a book or magazine, and there was a line at the check-out counter. I scanned the row of computers. I was in luck; one was unoccupied. I quickly logged on and typed up my resume. After ensuring it was mistake-free, I printed off a copy and paid my five cents. I reread my resume while I started the engine of my car. I was confident Josh would be impressed with my current employment and skills. I wondered if he had ever interviewed anyone my age who worked three jobs simultaneously. I hoped it was impressive and conveyed I was a hard worker.

On the drive home, I decided to project confidence during the interview, smile a lot, and be as personable as possible. I wanted to get out of my dismal financial situation and make a better life for myself and Heather.

# A Leap Of Faith

Kathy agreed to watch the children while I went to the interview. Thank goodness for dependable neighbors.

My resume was safely inside the pocket of an old school folder I found among my college books to keep it pristine and wrinkle-free. I placed the folder next to my purse on the kitchen table as a reminder to take it with me when I left. I popped a dish of leftovers in the oven to warm for dinner.

Opening the bifold doors of my closet, I chose my best blouse and skirt from my meager wardrobe and dressed, knowing I would have to apply my deodorant several times to control my sweaty armpits. After taking extra care to style my hair and makeup, I looked at my reflection in the full-length bedroom mirror that hung on the back of the door, satisfied with how I looked. Lipstick! I almost forgot.

    I hurried to the kitchen to retrieve my tube of lipstick and stopped short in the doorway. I stared at Heather, who sat in the center of the table with the contents of my purse scattered around her. She had opened my lipstick, and her face looked like a clown on an acid trip.

    "Oh, no. Heather, what did you do?"

    "Pretty." She smiled, quite proud of her artistry.

    Scanning the tabletop among the abstract lipstick drawing, I found what was left of my tube and put the top back on it. My heart skipped a beat when I noticed my folder and purse were missing. I scanned the floor and discovered both unscathed beneath the table and placed them on a chair. Sighing, a little disgusted and impatient knowing my time was limited, I grabbed a clean dishcloth from the kitchen drawer, dampened it with tap water, and drizzled it with dollar store dish soap. Heather read my intent. She scooted to the edge of the table, lowering her feet to a chair in her attempt to escape. As expected, she turned her head away from me while pushing against my arms and chest, trying to avoid a good face washing. I noticed her hands were also covered with lipstick and washed them clean before looking down at my blouse. Her precious handprints were painted in various mauve intensities on the fabric. After changing her into a clean outfit, I washed the kitchen table and quickly changed into my second-best blouse.

"Knock, knock," Kathy called as she entered my apartment.

I glanced at the clock on my nightstand. I needed to leave, or I would be late. I came out of the bedroom, fastening the last button of my blouse and tucking it into my skirt.

Kathy scanned my body from head to toe. "Oh, you look nice. Very professional."

"Thanks. I'm going to give it my best." I picked up the contents of my purse and put it back inside. "If Danny gets home before I do, dinner is in the oven. Thanks again for watching the kids." With my purse and resume in hand, I hurried to the door.

"No problem. Good luck."

Once in my van, I used my rearview mirror and applied my deformed lipstick. I imagined the questions Josh may ask and rehearsed what I thought were intelligent answers to convince him that I was the right person for the job. Unfamiliar with the industrial neighborhood, I allowed myself extra travel time to the office building. I prayed I would locate it with little difficulty and could sit in my van a moment or two to calm myself before going inside.

I pulled into the parking lot of a building that resembled a giant cube. It reminded me of a medical facility. Glancing at my watch, ten minutes to spare. I checked my hair and makeup in the rearview mirror, reached for the folder on the passenger seat, and sighed as I spotted a smudge of lipstick on the bottom front corner. I took my resume out of it and held the opposite ends together, careful not to fold it as I grabbed my purse and exited my van. I straightened my A-line skirt, ensured my bouse was tucked, and tugged at my restrained waist, remembering why I hated to wear nylons.

I took a deep breath and tilted my face toward the warm autumn sun as I walked the short distance to the double door entrance while saying a silent prayer. The trees surrounding the building had started changing into their fall wardrobe. Once inside, the contemporary lobby with its polished white floors, sterile-looking white walls, and plants in chrome planters seemed cold and unwelcoming. Since the office address began with a three, I needed to go to the third floor, pressed the up button for the elevator, and the awaiting doors opened. After pushing the third-floor button, it seemed like an

## A VICTIM OF DESPERATION

eternity until the elevator closed, and I watched the numbers illuminate as each floor was passed. It stopped with a jolt, the doors opened, and I exited to look over the railing at the atrium below. Impressive. A sign on the wall indicated the direction of the office I was seeking.

I stopped before a glass door and glanced at the number on the wall to verify I was at the correct office. I could see a man sitting behind a desk in the tiny room. The only item on the desk was a phone sitting in one corner. The walls were absent of pictures.

The man looked at me as I entered. He stood, dressed in a nice suit, clean-cut blonde hair, and blue eyes, the color of the ocean.

"May I help you?"

"Yes, I'm here for an interview. I'm Jess."

He scanned my body as if evaluating my worth. "Yes, we spoke on the phone. I'm Josh."

"It's nice to meet you in person, Josh." I extended my hand. After a courteous and quick handshake, he went to a door and knocked.

"Enter." A female voice replied.

Josh looked over his shoulder. "Follow me." He opened the door. "Jess is here to interview." He announced as he led me into a second tiny office.

The woman behind the desk failed to acknowledge my entrance as she continued to write in a file. I stood before a vacant chair and waited patiently. Her desk resembled a wooden table on legs with a piece of glass on top. I watched as Josh moved a chair from the wall, placed it on one end of the desk, and sat. The woman finished writing, closed the manila file, and pushed it aside. She smiled.

"I'm sorry to have kept you waiting. I'm Mrs. Smith."

I stepped forward, extending my hand. "Hi, I'm Jessica." I smiled, hoping to convey my confidence as we shook hands.

She reached for my resume, which I gave to her, and motioned to the chair behind me. "Please be seated."

I sat and waited while they read my resume together.

Mrs. Smith began. "So, Jessica, tell me about yourself."

I had anticipated the question. "I am eighteen, a single mom of a fifteen-month-old little girl, and I am currently working three jobs." After stating my rehearsed answer, it dawned on me that the information I conveyed was also written on my resume. Silly.

They both nodded approvingly.

Mrs. Smith's eyebrows drew together. "Who is watching your daughter now?"

## A VICTIM OF DESPERATION

"My neighbor, but my aunt watches her during the day when I work at the tanning salon. My boyfriend watches her in the evening when I work at the Coney."

"This job entails sales. Why do you want this job?"

"First, I think I can be an asset to your company. Second, I'm a people person, outgoing, and I have worked in sales before, that is, if you can call signing people up at the tanning salon and recommending food at the restaurant qualifying as sales. And third, I am looking to increase my income." I grinned, knowing my answer was professional and precise.

Both Josh and Mrs. Smith nodded their heads in agreement. She took two pieces of paper from her desk drawer and placed them before me on her desk.

"With your attitude, you will easily be able to earn checks like these."

I looked at the photocopies of the checks. The payable amounts were over $500.

She continued. "The checks were payment for one week of sales, but these two employees are aggressive and hard working. I get the impression you are equally as motivated."

I sat a little taller in the chair. "Yes, I am."

"Well," she began, "you seem perfect for the job." She looked at Josh for his opinion.

"I agree." He added.

"However," a sedate expression masked Mrs. Smith's face, "I just need to know…"

I wondered what barrage of questioning followed.

"…when can you start working?" She smiled.

I had not been told much about the job other than it involved sales. Monday? Was this another part-time job? I needed additional information before answering. "What days and hours are available?"

"Our sales staff works Tuesday through Saturday, eight to five."

I would have to give my notice to the tanning salon manager and inform my aunt. For the girls I babysit, maybe Kathy would like to watch them and make some extra money. If not, then their mother would need to find someone else. I could continue to work at the Coney in the evening.

"I can begin on Tuesday next week."

"Great." She took a piece of paper from a folder and handed it to me. "This is a job description of what you will be doing. Report here at eight in the morning on Tuesday to receive your first assignment. Dress comfortably and for the weather." She stood and extended her hand, as did Josh.

## A VICTIM OF DESPERATION

"Thank you. I'll see you in a week, next Tuesday." I shook their hands and left the office. Alone in the elevator, I jumped up and down and giggled. I knew my life was about to take a turn for the better. I was determined to earn the weekly paychecks like the copies they showed me—no more worrying about paying my bills.

I sat in my van and read the job description on the paperwork. I stared at the title 'Sales Engineer,' so basically a sales title. It sounded impressive, though.

## Determined To Succeed

I reported to the salon for work the next morning. I informed my aunt and manager I was leaving at the end of the week for a better opportunity.

"You are our most reliable employee. Your sales of tanning products consistently exceeded everyone else, and you always report to work on time. If you ever need a letter of recommendation, let me know." Before handing me my final paycheck, which included my commission, my aunt hugged me.

My hours would most likely be distributed to the other employees; whether they willingly accepted them was another issue. I decided to stay on at the restaurant

## A VICTIM OF DESPERATION

until I received a steady income from my new job. Kathy agreed to watch the children I babysat, which eased their mother's mind.

Danny left for work early on Monday morning, leaving Heather and me to spend the day together before I had to report to the restaurant in the evening.

The morning sun illuminated the colorful foliage on the trees, inviting us to enjoy its glorious display. I thought it would be a perfect day to take advantage of the warm autumn day and have a picnic lunch in the park. With our lunch packed, I put Heather in the umbrella stroller, and we walked to the park, played on the playground, and ate our lunch by the pond. I tossed several pieces of my bread crust on the ground toward the ducks nearest us. They waddled frantically toward the offering and raced after each tidbit I offered, fascinating Heather. I laughed as she crept close to them with the hope of holding one, but they scurried away, causing her to squeal with delight.

My customers at the restaurant were far and few between for the evening. Nothing like the chaos on all you can eat Wednesday night.

After a restless night of tossing and turning, my alarm clock seemed to ring much too early. I left Heather in my aunt's care and drove to the office building to report for the first day of my new job.

I took a deep breath as I stood outside the office door. Josh and two other people were standing in Mrs. Smith's office while I took a moment to finger-comb my wind-blown, mussy hair.

Josh looked over his shoulder as I opened the door to the office. He stepped to the open doorway and waved me forward. "Good morning, Jess. Come on in and meet everyone."

I followed him into the office where two other girls stood listening to Mrs. Smith speak from her chair like a queen on a throne. She looked at me, raised her arm, palm up, and signaled for me to come forward with the wave of her fingers. I stopped before her desk.

"And here is our latest associate sales rep. Ladies, this is Jessica. We just hired her last week."

I turned around to face the other two sales reps.

"Hi, Jessica." They greeted.

I smiled and waved as Mrs. Smith made the introduction.

"This is Sharon and Lucy. Josh is your leader, and he will drive each of you to your sales territory." She picked up the three piles of cardstock papers and handed one to each of us. "Your inventory has been counted. You will sell them for $20 each. When you return, you will turn in the money you collected, and your unsold inventory will be counted. You will be paid $5 for each one you sell, minus expenses. Are there any questions?"

I stood dumbfounded while I read the top paper, recognizing many of the businesses printed on the perforated rectangles. Coupons? Am I selling coupons?

Mrs. Smith continued after pausing a moment. "Good. Please, for your safety, do not reveal your name or any other personal information to customers. You are not to go inside their houses and keep the topic of conversation on selling and selling alone. Josh has your maps. I'll see you upon your return." She picked up a pen and a piece of paper from an open file in an unspoken dismissal.

The four of us were silent on the way down in the elevator and to Josh's car. I sat in the back seat with Lucy.

Josh turned in the driver's seat and handed each of us a map. "This is a map of the neighborhood you will be responsible for today. Each of you has a different one to cover. On your map is a circled intersection. That is where I will pick you up around five o'clock. As Mrs. Smith explained, we will return to the office to have your unsold inventory counted, submit the cash you collected, and receive your pay."

He started the ignition, drove us to each destination, and dropped off the other two girls before stopping at an intersection where I was to begin my day.

"Good luck, Jess. See you at five o'clock."

I watched him drive away. He expected me to sell coupons for eight hours? I guess I was to do without lunch today. I would have to pack one or stuff some snacks in my pockets for tomorrow. Maybe something to drink too.

I turned, looked at the neighborhood, and my mouth dropped open. Could anyone be living in these houses?

Trash littered the pothole-paved street. Many of the houses had peeling paint, missing shingles, boarded up windows, and overgrown lawns. The charred skeletal remains of a house pointed skyward like ribs of a carcass; its roof collapsed. It should have been torn down long ago. Where had Josh taken me?

Even though it was a sunny and warm day for autumn, a chill rippled up my spine. I doubted anyone living on this street could afford to spend money on coupons. I sighed and lifted my chin, determined to do my best. I examined the map, which only contained the neighborhood I was assigned. I had no way of knowing how far I was from home. I tried to orientate myself as I

## A VICTIM OF DESPERATION

turned the map one way, then the other to match the street corner where I was standing.

With my bearings established, I put the map in my back pocket, marched up to the first house, knocked on the door, and waited. I paused with my knuckled fist above the door as I heard the lock click. A little old man opened the door a mere crack.

"Good day, sir. I have coupons for sale, which will save you lots of money. They are only $20. How many of them would you like?"

"None." The door was slammed in my face.

I went to the next house and knocked. There was no answer. After several hours of going door to door, my stomach began to grumble, and my enthusiasm wane. I went to the next house, gave my rehearsed speech to a relatively robust woman, and waited for the rejection.

"So, tell me about these coupons. How do I use them?" The woman squinted at the sheet I held before her. Assuming she needed a pair of reading glasses, I placed a sheet of coupons in her hand, pointed at one, and explained the discount for that local restaurant. I also touched other coupons, explaining where they could be used, when they expired, and the price.

"All right. I'll take one. Let me get the money." She handed the sheet back to me before she disappeared from the doorway.

My mouth dropped open. My first sale?

The woman returned and gave me a $20 bill. I handed her the coupon sheet in exchange.

"Thank you. Have a good day." I turned and walked down the sidewalk with a spring in my step, my confidence renewed, and went to the next house.

I could tell by the placement of the sun that it was getting late in the day. I had forgotten to wear my watch, so I had no idea what time it was. I went to the next house, knocked on the door. A young woman carrying a baby on her hip answered.

"Hello, I am going door to door today with an opportunity for you to save money when dining out and at other services offered by businesses around town." I held up the sheet of coupons and pointed to the various offers. "The cost is $20, and you can easily receive a return on your meager investment by using only five of these coupons."

"No, thank you." She clasped the door's edge and began closing it.

"If you don't mind me asking. Do you know the time?"

The woman stepped back and leaned into an adjacent doorway, probably checking a clock on the stove. "It is 4:45."

## A VICTIM OF DESPERATION

"Thank you. Have a nice day." I hurried down the sidewalk and pulled the map out of my back pocket. I passed several houses, assuming their owners would be of little help to my day of dismal sales. I went directly to the nearest intersection. Realizing I was five blocks from the rendezvous point with Josh, I needed to hustle to make it on time. Would he leave without me if I were not there on time? I walked as fast as my tired legs could carry me while glancing at the map to ensure I was headed in the correct direction.

I saw Josh's car pull up to the designated pick-up spot and ran half a block to meet him. I sat in the back seat, tired, hungry, and out of breath.

He looked in the rearview mirror. "How did you do?" He checked for oncoming traffic before merging into the street.

It took a deep breath, trying to calm my thumping heart before I spoke. "I was hoping to do better, but I sold three."

He tilted his head to the side, and a fleeting frown conveyed his disappointment. "It's a start." His comment was void of encouragement.

We picked up Lucy and Sharon before returning to the office, where I turned in the unsold coupons and the money I collected to Mrs. Smith. I waited while she thumbed through my unsold coupons, and my collect money was verified. I watched as she scribbled something on a small scrap of paper and withdrew money from a cashbox.

"Here is your pay for today. Let's hope you do better tomorrow." She handed me the paper and money. "Next."

I stared at the money in my hand, frozen like a statue.

"Is there something wrong, Jessica?" Mrs. Smith looked at me over the rim of her reading glasses as she reached for the unsold coupons Lucy handed her.

Realizing my mouth was open, I snapped it shut before looking at her. "What about the written check you showed me during the interview?" I blinked several times. "I guess I am surprised to be paid in cash today and not at the end of the week with a check."

"No, you are paid at the end of each day. The note explains your pay." She turned her attention away from me dismissively and began counting Lucy's coupons.

I exited her small office. Did she state that in the interview? I must have forgotten. I looked down at the ten dollars in my hand and read the note. I earned five dollars for each coupon sheet I sold. Gas? She deducted five dollars for gas. I could have driven myself.

## A VICTIM OF DESPERATION

I stopped before the office glass door and re-read the note.

Josh watched me from behind his desk. "Is there something wrong, Jess?"

I went to his desk and kept my voice just above a whisper so Mrs. Smith could not hear what I said. "Why did she deduct for gas? I have my car. I can drive myself."

"She wants to ensure you won't take off with the unsold coupons, sell them, and keep all of the money for yourself."

I looked at the piece of paper again. Federal or state tax deductions were absent. It dawned on me then, I had not filled out any tax forms.

Josh went on to explain. "You will be going to a different neighborhood tomorrow. Hopefully, your sales will improve. See you at eight o'clock."

I nodded once before leaving the office, drove to my aunt's house, and picked up Heather, who greeted me with open arms. Strange, I was comforted by someone so small as her tiny arms wrapped around my neck. I promised my aunt I would pay her thirty dollars a day by week's end.

I was able to spend a half-hour with my little girl while I prepared spaghetti for dinner. As Danny walked into the apartment, I walked out the door on my way to the restaurant. Tuesdays were usually relatively slow, but I would put in my hours and hope for a better than the usual amount in tips.

~

I arrived at the office the next morning to discover only Josh greeted us. I stood silently and listened to him speak.

"Let's set a goal for today. I want each of you to be a bellringer. How do you be a bellringer? Well, sell ten coupon sheets, and you can ring this bell when you return!" Josh picked up a bell from Mrs. Smith's desk and rang it loud and clear. Lucy clapped her hands and hopped up and down. He set the bell down, scooped up the pre-counted coupons, and gave us each a stack with a map.

As before, he dropped me off in an unfamiliar neighborhood. The houses looked even more rundown than the one I was in yesterday.

Dressed in jeans and a nice sweatshirt, I was better prepared for the long day. I carried a plastic grocery bag with a sandwich, an apple, and a bottle of water. I wished I would have packed an umbrella too, as I looked at the threatening sky. I knocked on the door of the first house.

## A VICTIM OF DESPERATION

My stomach began to grumble around noon. I sat on a curb and ate my lunch as the threatening clouds began to shed droplets of rain. Determined to reach the goal of selling ten coupon sheets, I put the empty water bottle in the front pocket of my sweatshirt, placed the plastic bag over my head, and went to the next house.

By the end of the day, I was drenched, shivering, and prayed I did not get sick. My sales were worse than yesterday. The accruing unpaid balances of my bills weighed heavily on my mind. Even though I was tired, I had to get through a long evening at the restaurant before my day would end. It was 'all you can eat conies and fries' night, our busiest day of the week. At least my tips would be decent.

On Friday, I pushed myself, determined to be a bellringer, and sold eleven coupon sheets. Once back at the office, I received my pay, minus gas money, and rang the bell. It was a proud moment, but was it worth my time away from Heather? It was Jim's scheduled weekend with her. At least Danny or Kathy would not have to watch her tomorrow while I worked.

I gave my baby girl a big hug and kiss when I picked her up. Thank goodness the tips I received from the restaurant were above average, and I could pay my aunt in full.

I had the evening off from the restaurant, which allowed me to be home when Jim came to pick Heather up for the weekend. I bathed her after dinner, dressed her in pajamas, packed her weekend bag, and placed it by the door when the phone rang.

"Hello."

"Hi, I can't come and get Heather. I am working this weekend." A flimsy excuse by Jim.

I shook my head. Typical. "Well, I'm working too."

"Maybe next weekend. I have to go." The receiver went dead. I rolled my lips inward as I stared at the receiver before handing it up on the cradle.

Heather was playing with her toys as I sat down at the kitchen table to pay my bills. To say I was scrimping by was an understatement. I crossed off the last day on the calendar and flipped the page to the next month. October, in all its colorful splendor, was here. I flipped back a page as a thought came to mind. Maybe my successful day of selling coupons was because it was payday for most people, and they had the cash to spend.

Knowing my aunt would not watch Heather on the weekends, I called Kathy.

"Hello."

I could hear her children playing in the background. "Hey, I have to work tomorrow, and Jim can't take Heather for the weekend. If Danny must work, can you watch her until I get home?"

"Sure, no problem."

"Thanks, I owe you."

I fell asleep before Danny arrived home from the bar. After all, it was Friday, the night to celebrate the week's end.

Danny and Heather were asleep as I dressed the next morning to report to Mrs. Smith's office. I scribbled a note to inform him Kathy was available to watch Heather if he had to go into work. I left the message on the kitchen table and grabbed my packed lunch as I left the apartment.

# Trudging On

At the end of the second week of hustling coupons, I was driven back to the office to turn in my sales. I had managed to ring the bell twice during my short employment. For some reason, Mrs. Smith's face was stern as she handed me my pay.

"Your sales are falling short of our expectations. You should easily be able to sell all twenty coupon sheets we give you each day. So, we are moving you to a more affluent neighborhood next week and hope your sales improve. If they do not, we would like you to consider going out of state for additional training."

## A VICTIM OF DESPERATION

My mouth dropped open as my eyebrows drew together. "Out of state? I can't leave my daughter."

"Well, let's hope your sales improve, and it won't be necessary."

My self-esteem collapsed like a deflated balloon. A pang of guilt pierced my heart. So much of my time away from Heather and I hardly anything to show for it.

I made a peanut butter and jelly sandwich for my daughter and me to share for dinner. Danny would have to make his meal tonight when he arrived home. I needed to change into my waitress outfit that reeked of fried food no matter how many times I washed it and get to the restaurant for another slow night with little money to show for it.

Exhausted, I arrived home after work to a dark apartment. Danny must have gone to bed early. I turned on the kitchen light and tiptoed to the bedroom to check on Heather in her crib, but it was empty. Danny was not in our bed either. My heartbeat quickened. Could he have her out this late at night? Where were they? I hurried to the kitchen and picked up the receiver of the phone to call Kathy. As I dialed the number, I heard a tapping on my door. I opened it to see Heather in Kathy's arms.

"I heard your door slam shut—those dang spring hinges. Danny asked me to watch Heather. He went out for the evening." She carried my sleeping child toward the bedroom.

I stood dumbfounded as I closed the door. "Danny went out?"

"Yes, said he was tired of sitting home alone and went to the bar." She whispered over her shoulder as she laid Heather in her crib.

My heart thumped in my chest as my blood pressure increased. I get it. Danny needs to go out every so often for a beer with the guys, but he could have left a note. Kathy came back into the living room.

I tried to smile even though I was seething inside. "I hope Heather wasn't an imposition."

Kathy chuckled. "No, she is a delight. She is becoming quite a regular at our place. Good night."

I walked Kathy to the door. "Thanks for watching her. Good night." I stood transfixed as I watched the door close, and my mind began to race. A regular? Damn. How many times a week was he going out instead of watching Heather? I had a suspicion this was not the first time. He must have been able to return from an outing before I arrived home from work.

I tried to stay calm, but here I was, busting my butt to make enough money to pay my bills while he's going to bars and paying top dollar for watered-down drinks? I understand he needs to get out once and a while, but he could have let me know instead of sneaking around behind my back.

I was too angry to sleep. It was past two in the morning when I heard the apartment door open and slam shut. After listening to Danny pee a river in the bathroom, he came into the bedroom, stripped down to his underwear, and got into bed.

"Late night?" The sarcasm in my voice was clearly detectable, but in his intoxicated state, I doubted he was capable of recognizing the angry tone of my voice.

He rolled toward me. I wrinkled my nose at the pungent rankness of the alcohol on his breath and cigarette smoke in his hair.

"Later than normal." He admitted. His words were slurred.

"Normal? You mean you do this regularly?" I sat up in bed and crossed my arms over my chest, aghast by his admission.

"Ya, usually two or three times a week. Heather is fine. Kathy always watches her."

He was running around at night instead of watching Heather and taking advantage of Kathy for his selfish purpose. In his intoxicated state, it was pointless to argue with him. He probably would not remember what was said anyway. I snuggled beneath the blankets, rolled away from him, and vowed to discuss the subject with him in the morning. Thank goodness I had the day off because I had an inkling our discussion on the matter would be in-depth and lengthy.

# Potential And Disappointment

Our discussion did not go as I planned. Danny argued for his need to have a social life and defensively insisted on doing as he wanted. I understood his point of view. After all, Heather was not his child. I expressed my gratitude for the times he watched Heather. However, I thought it was inappropriate for him to take advantage of Kathy by dumping my daughter on her so often. In the end, he apologized and promised to stay home during the week to watch Heather. If Kathy were available, he insisted on going out both Friday and Saturday nights. Was I jealous of his carefree life? His lack of responsibility?

It took a few minutes for me to self-analyzing and determine the reason for my hurt feelings. Danny had time for his friends, but no time to spend with me. Was that my fault? I had little choice in the hours I worked. Couldn't he stay home, plan a romantic evening, and spend time with me?

When Mrs. Smith handed me my pay at week's end, she also gave me an additional slip of paper.

"We are moving the office to a new location. Report to this address on Tuesday."

Moving the office? Maybe the lease had expired, but I thought it strange it would do so midway through the month. I stared at the new address as I left the office. The street was unfamiliar to me. Maybe Danny knew where it was located.

~

I pulled my van alongside the curb, put it into park, and stared at the Victorian house with a wraparound porch as I reported to work the following week. I expected an office building. I checked the paper to make sure I was at the correct address and glanced at my wrist to check the time. I scanned the enormous house as I walked up the sidewalk to the front door. Was that a sheet in one window and clothes hanging on hangers in another? It resembled a halfway house that rented rooms. I stepped onto the porch and knocked on the door.

Josh answered. "Hello, Jessica. Right on time."

Once through a foyer, I entered a large living room with its walls decorated with an elaborate floral wallpaper and crown molding framing the top, making a large square on the high ceiling. I could hear Mrs. Smith lecturing the small crowd of salespeople, a mix of young men and women. I did not see Lucy but spotted Sharon on the other side of the room.

Mrs. Smith saw me enter and silently encouraging me to join the others with a wave of her hand. She called someone's name, and they stepped forward to join her.

"We have a bellringer here!" She held up a bell and presented it to the guy, who rang the bell while everyone clapped. He handed the bell back to Mrs. Smith, who continued. "Please remember, for your safety, you are not to reveal your name or any other personal information to the customers, and you are not to go inside their houses. Now, I know we are all going to have a successful day. Let's clap it out!"

Everyone began to clap while chanting something I could not understand.

Josh began handing out stacks of coupons as the noise quieted.

"As you know, you will be driven to different territories today, and we expect your sales to improve." Mrs. Smith began handing out coupons as well.

Even though it was bold of me to do so, I had to voice my opinion as Josh handed me my stack. "In all honesty, the neighborhoods we were assigned in the past were rather rundown. The people had no money to spare, except on payday. I'm surprised I sold any coupons at all."

Josh paused with a stack of coupons in his hand. "That is a very astute analysis, Jess. Unfortunately, we need to drive a greater distance to get you to the new neighborhood. It will cut your selling time by about an hour since we must be back here by five o'clock too. I hope you put on your running shoes because you will have to hustle to sell all twenty coupons today. I will be with you as soon as I distribute the rest of these." He called several other people's names and gave them their coupons while I waited near the doorway and watched them exit the house.

The room was nearly empty when Josh passed by me with the maps in hand, and I followed him to his car with two other people I did not know in tow. We drove for quite some time, and I studied the coupons to familiarize myself with the businesses printed on them. After dropping off the other two associates, I was delivered to my sales territory. Josh handed me a map.

"I'll pick you up at 4:30 at the circled intersection. Be on time. We will need to hurry back and hopefully won't get stuck in rush hour traffic."

I nodded, got out of the car, and looked at my watch for the time. It was 9:30. A glance at houses along the street caused me to groan internally. Another run-down neighborhood? Maybe even worse than my last territory. I hurried to the first house and knocked.

An old woman dressed in a dirty nightgown answered. Her gray hair was thin, greasy, and looked like it had been weeks since she had combed it. Anticipating a rejection, I wanted to turn around, but I had set a goal to sell all twenty of my coupon sheets. I smiled.

"Good morning."

"Is it?" The old woman scowled.

"I like to think so." I held up one of the coupon sheets. "I have an opportunity for you to save money."

"That means you want me to spend money. No, thanks." She slammed the door in my face.

Since my time was limited, I cut across the lawn to the next house to find the windows and door covered with plywood. I quickened my steps, distancing myself from the creepy house, determined to cover the entire territory by pick-up time.

I did my best to promote, convince, and sell while projecting an upbeat mood. By the time I had to meet Josh, I had only sold one coupon sheet. When I turned in my day's work to Mrs. Smith, she counted the unsold sheets, scribbled on a piece of paper, and handed me the note. Ten dollars had been deducted for gas.

"Ten?"

Mrs. Smith scowled. "Yes, more gas was used to drive you further. The remaining five dollars you owe for gas will be taken out of tomorrow's sales."

I stared at her, unable to comprehend what she said. What if I could not sell any tomorrow?

She sighed. "It's your fault. You need more training. Next."

I was dismissed.

After picking up Heather, I arrived home and made a nice dinner for the three of us. I had the night off from the restaurant and was looking forward to spending time with Danny.

He arrived home to discover the table set and dinner ready to eat.

"Wow, what's the special occasion?" He sat and began filling his plate with food.

## A VICTIM OF DESPERATION

"I have the night off from the Coney. I thought I would make dinner, and we could watch a movie after Heather was in bed for the night."

"It looks delicious, but I'm going out with the guys tonight."

The expression on my face went from a glowing smile to a frown of utter disappointment. "But it's Tuesday. You said you would only go out on Fridays and Saturdays. Dang, how many nights a week do you go out with the guys while I am working my butt off?"

"Usually, three times a week. Sometimes more." He shrugged his shoulder as I glared at him. "Hey, it's no fun being here by myself while the baby sleeps. It's nice to talk to another adult once and a while. Besides, Kathy is always next door to cover for me."

"I don't think you should take advantage of her like that, and I depend on you to watch Heather. I know she is safe when she is with you."

"She is safe with Kathy."

"That's not the point."

"Well, tonight you can be with her because I am going out."

We ate our meal in silence. I washed the dishes while Danny took a shower. As I was busy drying and putting them away in the cupboard, he kissed me on the cheek and left.

Dejected, I sat on the floor and played with Heather before bathing, reading a story, and putting her down for the night.

Nothing appealed to me on the television, so I took a shower and went to bed. I had to return to the dilapidated neighborhood for another long day tomorrow and work in the evening at the restaurant for 'all you can eat' night. I closed my eyes, hoping my sleep would not be interrupted when Danny came home.

~

I turned in my meager sales each day, only to be lectured on how it was my fault my sales were low, I needed to do better, and by receiving additional training, my sales would improve. I even had a few days when I did not sell any coupons, yet I still owed the gas expense. I wondered if Mrs. Smith and Josh knew the neighborhood would generate low sales, thus pushing me toward going out of state to receive more training, or was it a test to gauge my ability as a salesperson?

After working in the new location for two weeks, Josh picked me up at Saturday's designated intersection. I squirmed in the backseat knowing the reflection of his eyes in the rearview mirror stared at me.

## A VICTIM OF DESPERATION

Defying his inquisitive stare, I looked at the mirror, unflinching.

"Jess, did you do any better today?"

I thumbed through the remaining unsold coupons. There were seventeen. "About the same."

"You know, Jess, it may be time for you to think about traveling further away for sales."

I had heard the same suggestion many times over. "I know, out of state."

"I think you should consider it. You can make more money."

I sighed and looked out the window. "I can't. I have a baby. She is only sixteen-months old. Plus, since I have yet to make much money at this job, I have a second job that I work nights and weekends to pay my bills."

"Well, think it over. I think you should consider it."

I had worked for the company a month, put in long hours without much to show for it. I knew I could reach the five hundred dollars a week if given the right neighborhood. I did not want to leave my baby girl. I did not want to quit my job at the Coney. I remained silent the entire ride to the house, checked in, and received five dollars.

Josh's words echoed in my mind as I drove my beat-up van to my aunt's house. I knew I could depend on her to watch Heather if I went out of state. Could I trust Danny to spend time with her in the evening, or would he dump my daughter onto Kathy while he went to the bar nearly every night?

I had the night off from the restaurant, so when Danny arrived home for dinner, I wanted his opinion on the proposed opportunity.

"How was work?" I thought it best to start with small talk as I cut up a canned peach wedge for Heather and placed it on the highchair tray.

"The usual." He shoveled a forkful of spaghetti in his mouth.

"Mine was slow. It has been since they moved me to the new neighborhood."

He continued to chew, so I went on.

"They say I need additional training."

"Oh." Danny bit into a slice of garlic bread.

"The training is out of state." That caught his attention.

He stopped chewing and stared at me. "Out of state? A business trip, so to speak. Where?"

"I don't know."

"For how long?"

"I don't know that either."

"When are you going?"

## A VICTIM OF DESPERATION

"I'm not, well, not yet." With my fork in hand, I pushed the spaghetti around my plate. "I know I can make lots of money in this job, but they keep assigning me to poor neighborhoods. Maybe I do need more training. I don't know." I looked at Heather and watched as she shoved a handful of spaghetti in her mouth. I smiled at her cheeks painted with sauce, knowing she would resist me washing her face.

"I think you need more information. If you need to go, then go. I can take Heather to your aunt's house in the morning and watch her at night."

"What about you going out to the bar at night?"

"What about it? I deserve a night off once and a while."

"Once and a while? You go out three or more times a week."

"Kathy watches her while I am out."

"Do you pay her?"

"No."

"It's not right to take advantage of her generosity."

"She doesn't mind." He twirled his fork in the spaghetti swirling the noodles into a mound.

"The point is, I do. I need you here watching Heather. I need to know she will be safe while I'm gone."

"Then I guess you are just going to have to trust me. I'm not an idiot, and I know how to take care of her."

Maybe that was my issue. I did not trust Danny. Perhaps I did not like it when he went out having a good time drinking with his friends. Maybe I was jealous because he had time for his friends and preferred to be with them when I had a night off work. I can't remember the last time he suggested the two of us do something together. If I could make enough money so I would not have to work as much, perhaps we would have more time to spend together. I was trapped, unable to keep the apartment without him paying for half of the expenses.

I looked at Danny and spoke my mind. "I would appreciate it if you wouldn't go out so much and you were here with her."

He did not reply.

~

I sat at the table and stared at the stack of bills I was unable to pay. Emptying my tip jar, the coins bounced onto the tabletop. I had enough to put gas in the van and pick up a few groceries from the dollar store. I did not want to leave Heather, but my hand was being forced, and I would inevitably have to do so. I called Mr.

## A VICTIM OF DESPERATION

West and informed him of Jim's failure to pay child support. He said he would remind my ex to do so, but I knew the results would be the same. I finally called Jim, who lived with his parents.

"Hello." Jim's dad answered the phone.

"Hello, this is Jessica. Is Jim there?"

"No. Did you need him for anything, in particular, Jess?"

"I need him to pay his child support." My request was met by silence. I went on to explain. "He has yet to make one payment."

"I'll see that you get it."

"Thank you."

I received a check in the mail five days later, assuming Jim's enabling parents had sent Mr. West the money. It was enough to tide me over for a few weeks, I hoped.

I dressed Heather as a bunny for Halloween, and we visited both of my parents' neighborhoods. I giggled as my daughter's tail wiggled back and forth as she walked along the sidewalk carrying her plastic pumpkin basket and visited each house to collect candy. It wasn't long before she resembled a chipmunk with her cheeks filled with candy, and she became a sticky mess.

November seemed to pass quickly as I ran myself ragged between two jobs, keeping the apartment clean, the laundry caught up, and spending time with Heather. My success at selling coupons depended on the type of neighborhood and if it was a payday weekend.

With several pumpkin pies in hand, we traveled between households for Thanksgiving. The three of us arrived at Dad's house for a simple dinner, then to my mom's house, where Danny's family joined us for another dinner. It was nice to have the day off from work and be in the company of family, and unfortunately, the last time I would see them for a while.

# Making The Decision

Most of my knocks on front doors were unanswered over the next two days causing coupon sales to be dismally low. I guessed many of the owners were shopping at the malls and taking advantage of Black Friday and Saturday sales in preparation for Christmas. How was I going to pay for gifts for the holiday?

I arrived at the house office on Tuesday morning and pulled Josh aside.

"I have decided to go out of state. Even though I have had a few bellringer days, I have yet to meet my daily quota. I need more training."

He nodded as he grinned. "Jess, that's good to hear. I'm confident your sales will improve with some training. Let me speak to Mrs. Smith and see when it will begin." He disappeared into the adjacent room and emerged moments later. "She said in three days. There will be two others joining us for the trip."

My eyebrows were raised in question. "Two? Us?"

"Yes, I will be driving the three of you there."

It eased my mind knowing he would be going with me. "Um, where will we be going for the training?"

"Tennessee. You won't need to bring any money with you, just clothes and necessities."

Tennessee? I had never traveled out of state before. I was glad I did not have to take money out of my savings account, but I would bring what little I had in the tip jar, just in case.

On my last evening at the restaurant, I informed my boss I had to go out of town for training, but I hoped to return to work once I finished. He scowled at my nonchalant announcement but indicated he would hold my job open for me.

Once home, I packed most of my summer clothes while Danny watched TV. Even though it was the end of November, the weather would be similar to Florida's warm temperatures.

## A VICTIM OF DESPERATION

I stared at Heather as she slept in her crib. A tear cascaded down my cheek. I reached through the bars and cupped her chubby face in the palm of my hand. "I have to leave tomorrow night. I will be gone for a while, but I'll be home as soon as I can, baby girl. I promise." I traced my finger over her soft cheek and under her chin. "I love you." I sighed before climbing into my bed.

I rose early to spend some extra time with Heather before dropping her off with my aunt, going to the house office, and stood, listing to the empty promises of Mrs. Smith.

Josh stepped to my side and leaned toward me. "Are you packed and ready to leave tonight?"

I nodded, unwilling to speak.

"Good. I'll follow you home and pick you up from there."

"I have to stop at my aunt's house to pick up my daughter first. Can you pick me up at 6:00? My boyfriend should be home by then so he can watch her." He probably knew my address from my resume on file.

Josh hesitated for a moment. "I hadn't planned on leaving that late, but sure."

With my coupons and map in hand, he once again drove me to a rundown neighborhood and dropped me off at an intersection. I hurried to the first house with a mental goal of selling as many as possible, so I would have the extra money in my pocket for the training in Tennessee.

I did not have a bellringer day, but I came close. I collected my pay, minus the gas expense. A heaviness settled within my heart as I picked up Heather and hugged her while holding back my tears. I placed her on my hip and looked at my aunt.

"I have to go out of town for training for my job. Danny will be dropping off and picking up Heather while I am gone. Here is what I owe you for this week." I pulled the money from my back pocket and handed it to her.

Concern masked my aunt's face. "How long will you be gone?"

"I don't know. Hopefully, not more than a few days." I looked at Heather, and my bottom lip quivered. "I don't want to be away from her, but if this will further my career, then it is for the best." I kissed my baby girl's cheek and looked at my aunt. "I know I can depend on you to care for her while I am gone."

"Absolutely. Heather is a joy to watch."

"Thank you." I hugged my aunt, conveying my gratefulness, before leaving and driving home.

I popped a frozen pan of lasagna in the oven for dinner and dumped a can of green beans into a pan to heat on the stovetop. I sat on the floor and played with Heather casting her antics, facial expression, and every word she babbled to my mind. Even though I hoped to be gone only a few days, the thought of separation from my daughter pulled at my heartstrings.

Danny walked in the door as I set dinner on the table. The clock on the stove indicated I had twenty minutes before Josh arrived. I scooped a spoonful of lasagna and beans onto Heather's plate, cut it into small pieces, and placed it in the freezer to cool quickly.

"What time are you leaving?" Danny sat and filled his plate.

"In about twenty minutes."

"Are you packed?"

"Yes." I retrieved Heather's food, touched it to ensure it was cooled, and placed it on her highchair tray. I grabbed her small fork from the kitchen drawer and handed it to her even though I knew she would get frustrated and used her hand anyway.

"Do you know how long you will be away?" He shoveled a forkful of lasagna into his mouth.

"They didn't give me a date. It should be only a few days, a week at most." I sighed, trying to keep my tears in check. "There should be a phone I can use, so I will try to call you every day."

He simply nodded as he shoved another forkful into his mouth.

My stomach was jumbled in knots, and I could hardly sit still. This was a big step for me. I managed to eat what little I had put on my plate. Heather was a slow eater, so I knew I would have to leave before she finished. I picked up her fork from the highchair tray and poked it into a tiny piece of lasagna.

'Here, baby girl." I unconsciously opened my mouth, mirroring her as she resembled a baby bird awaiting the morsel of food I offered.

Unable to eat, I took my plate to the sink and glanced at the stove clock. Five minutes. I didn't want Josh to wait for me, so I grabbed my packed bag from the bedroom and placed my keys on the dresser for Danny to use my van if needed. I jerked my lightweight jacket from the hanger in the closet, set my items by the apartment door, and took a deep breath, hoping to keep my composure while I said good-bye.

"Well, I have to go." I stood next to Danny's chair.

He rose, hugged, and kissed me. "Call when you can, and don't worry, we will be just fine."

"I will. Love you."

"Love you too."

I turned to Heather. As expected, she had given up on her fork and proceeded to shove fistfuls of lasagna and green beans into her mouth, covering both cheeks as well. I wanted to pick her up, squeeze her tightly to my chest, silently letting her know how much I loved her, but the last thing I needed was tomato sauce staining my shirt. She reached her arm toward me. I clasped it by the wrist and kissed it. I pressed my lips against her temple near her hair, inhaling her baby shampoo scent. "Bye, baby girl. Momma will be back soon. I love you."

She waved her hand. "Bye, bye."

I turned away before my welling tears fell onto my cheeks, grabbed my bag and coat, and left the apartment.

Josh pulled into the parking lot as I exited the building. He hopped out of the car and popped the trunk. "Right on time." He accepted my bag and put it in the trunk as I slipped on my jacket to shield me from the chilly evening air.

"Yep." My reply was curt. I did not want him to detect the sadness in my voice and my current state of mind. What was my state of mind? Fear? Apprehension? Guilt for leaving Heather? For her sake, I needed to stay focused on my goal, which was to go through the training and return home as quickly as possible.

He slammed the trunk shut. "I already picked up the other two girls. There is an open seat in the back."

I got into the backseat and looked at the girl beside me. Her big blue eyes looked at me, and she smiled. She had long blonde hair, thick and straight, and was strikingly beautiful. She looked younger than me. I could not recall seeing her at the house office. An oversight on my part? The girl who sat in the front seat wore her brunette hair in a sloppy bun.

    Josh pulled out of the parking lot, and we headed south.

# Southward Bound

With my seatbelt fastened, I exhaled, forcing myself to relax as the distance between Heather and me lengthened. I was doing this for the both of us, right? I wish I had a cell phone to call and check on her, but the monthly bill exceeded my budget. I prayed there was a phone I could use at our destination, wherever that may be.

The silence in the car hung in the air like a thick fog. Josh had grown uncomfortable with the lack of conversation and turned on the radio keeping the volume low. The familiar music helped to distract my mind. I looked out the window as we left the city and headed into the countryside. It was mostly farmland, dotted with horses and cows. Many of the fields had been harvested. Before long, the sun dipped below the horizon, and a blanket of darkness covered the landscape.

"I have to get gas, so this is a good time for you to use the bathroom and grab a bite to eat." Josh pulled off the expressway and into a gas station.

Even though I was told not to bring cash, I was thankful I did. The other two passengers went into the gas station as Josh took his wallet from his back pocket of his pants and pulled out some money. Why didn't he have a company credit card to pay for the gas?

I pealed seven dollars off the bills I kept folded in my back pocket. "Here, to help pay for gas."

He stared at the money I offered momentarily before accepting it. "Thanks, Jess. I appreciate it."

I went into the gas station, used the restroom, and bought a granola bar and a bottle of water while cursing myself for not having the foresight to bring snacks from the dollar store instead of spending too much money on the overpriced items.

Rejoining everyone at the car, Josh merged onto the expressway. I sat silently in the back seat and read each state sign as we crossed its border.

## A VICTIM OF DESPERATION

After several stops for gas, food, and bathroom breaks, we exited onto a deserted road somewhere in Tennessee.

Josh pulled into the well-lit parking lot of the apartment complex. The three-story-high colonial-style building looked well maintained. I stepped out of the car into the night air, colder than I expected.

Surrounded by trees on a moonless night, the building appeared to be in the middle of nowhere. I could not hear the traffic of the expressway. I did not see a convenience store, gas station, or strip mall. What if there was a medical emergency? What if I needed a tampon? Did I remember to pack any tampons?

We unloaded the trunk, followed Josh into the building, and climbed the stairs to the second floor.

He stopped before an apartment and unlocked the door. "Home sweet home." He motioned for the other girls and me to proceed before him.

My skin prickled with gooseflesh as I entered. I curled my upper lip as the sensation of my body being submerged into a tub of cloudy-gray bathwater with lice floating on its surface made me second guess my decision to go out of state. Something was wrong. Something was terribly wrong. The hair on the back of my neck rose, and a shiver went up my spine.

I passed by the open doorway to the unlit kitchen on my left and stood in the dimly lit living room, or what I thought was the living room. It was void of furniture. I scanned the bodies of fifteen to twenty people lying on the floor. Many were asleep.

"Hey, Sam." Josh greeted.

A rather large man emerged from a hallway. "You made it." He glanced at the other girls and me. "More recruits?"

"Yes, this is Jessica." He motioned toward me, and Sam stepped forward.

"Hello, Jessica." He extended his hand. Hesitant, I placed mine in his. He covered it with his other hand, trapping mine in between.

"Hi." I wanted to withdraw my hand but did not want to appear impolite. The seconds ticked by, and I shifted my duffle bag higher on my shoulder before he finally withdrew his hands, releasing mine.

Josh introduced the other two girls. Sam asked to speak with him once we were settled and retreated down the hallway.

I looked at Josh. "So, where do I sleep?"

"You can throw your bag anywhere there isn't a body. As you can see, everyone sleeps on the floor. Well, all except Sam. He has the only bedroom and a private bathroom. The bathroom you will use is just down the hall." Josh walked away, and I followed him into the kitchen as he flipped on the overhead light. He opened the refrigerator door, discovered it was empty, and shut the door.

I looked at the wall in the kitchen, assuming a phone would be there. I did not see one. Maybe it was in Sam's room. I sidestepped toward Josh and kept my voice at a whisper. "I don't like this place. It gives me the creeps. I want to go home."

"Jess, you just got here. Give it a chance, a few days. I promise you will be able to make more in sales here than at home."

I thought of Heather, most likely asleep in her crib. Did she miss me? Did she even realize I was gone? Dismayed, I stepped into the living room that was wall to wall bodies. I went to the adjoining dining room. Thank goodness it was void of furniture too. I set my bag in the corner and plopped onto the floor. The two girls who arrived with me did the same. I watched as Josh went into the hallway where Sam had disappeared. The sound of a can opening echoed down the hallway. Were they drinking beer? Did Sam have a refrigerator in his room? I listened to their murmured conversation as it drifted into the room. I knew Josh was my 'leader,' and Sam was playing the role of Mrs. Smith.

I sighed. It had been a long day, both physically and emotionally. I laid on the floor, covered myself with my jacket, and used my duffle bag as a pillow. I closed my eyes, hoping to find solace while sleeping before facing the challenges of tomorrow.

# In A Strange Place

"Get up! Time to get going!" Came a booming voice.

My eyes fluttered open. I blinked several times before the blurriness cleared, and I was able to focus on Josh lying next to me. Was he ensuring I remained safe and untouched by others during the night? What day is it? Saturday, I think.

"Let's go!" Sam clapped his hands. "Donuts and juice are in the kitchen." He disappeared into his room as a line for the only bathroom began.

"God, what time is it?" I sat up and stared at the commotion of people scurrying about the room. Some stood in line for the bathroom while others herded like cattle toward the kitchen to eat.

Josh checked his cell phone. "Seven in the morning."

"Why are we up so early?" I finger-combed my hair, quite sure I had a bad case of bedhead.

"It takes that long for everyone to use the bathroom, eat, and receive their instructions before going to work."

My head snapped toward him. "Work? Selling coupons?"

He sat up. "Yes."

My eyebrows drew together, nearly forming a unibrow. Did I hear Josh correctly? "What about my training?"

"It will come with time." He went to the tiny kitchen to grab a donut and juice before the room became a chaotic melee.

I retrieved my cosmetic bag, toiletries, and a change of clothes from my duffle bag. I doubted I would have time for a shower as I took my place at the end of the line for the bathroom.

I waited and watched as each person exited and headed toward the kitchen. Most of the associates were women, but there were a few guys. Many looked to be about my age, between sixteen and nineteen. I looked at Josh as he finished off a second donut and emptied his paper cup of juice.

The bathroom door opened, and a redheaded gal exited. I closed the door behind me as I entered and locked it. The room reeked of urine, body odor, and god knows what else. I fought the urge to gag as I stared at the stained toilet bowl and wondered when it was last cleaned. Toilet paper littered the floor. I was thankful there was still some on the roll for me to use.

Unable to withstand the untidiness, I used a square of toilet paper to pick up the scraps on the floor and put it on top of the overflowing trash can before stamping it down with my flipflop. The sink was streaked with white, blue, and green toothpaste. I grabbed another wad of toilet paper, dampened it, and cleaned the sink before brushing my teeth. I changed into clean underwear, a pair of shorts, and a tank top. With a quick make-up job and my hair pulled into a ponytail, I exited, tucked my items and dirty clothes in my bag, and went to the kitchen to find the donut boxes empty. I poured myself the remaining half glass of orange juice and turned to see Josh watching me from the doorway.

"Now you know why I get in line for donuts and juice before using the bathroom." He grinned, showing his pearly white straight teeth.

"You could have advised me to do the same."

He ignored my comment. "Come on, the meeting is about to begin."

I slammed down the juice, tossed my cup in the trashcan, and sat at the rear of the group staring up at Sam, who towered over us.

"Good morning. We have new members joining us from another state today. Can each of you stand?" He motioned with his hand for the three of us to rise.

I stood defiantly, lifting my chin, and looked him directly in the eye. I did not like the situation I was in. I had been coerced, tricked, fooled, or whatever you want to call it. I remained unsmiling. I would get home one way or another, and soon.

He began clapping, and the group joined him. "Welcome. Glad to have you with us."

I sat as the greeting subsided, and he continued.

"You all know what to do. Do not tell your customers your name or anything personal about you. Do not go into their houses. You will be given twenty coupon sheets. If any of them are unaccounted for upon your return, it will come out of your pay. Now, you will be taken to a rather affluential neighborhood today. We will begin transporting at eight-thirty so you can be at your destination by nine. You will be picked up at sundown, so you should have plenty of time to sell all twenty of your coupons. I'm quite confident all of you will return and ring the bell today."

I felt a tap on the shoulder and turned to see Josh behind me.

"The three of you will ride with me instead of taking the van." He looked at the other two girls ensuring they heard him.

I nodded once as I accepted my twenty coupons and a map from Sam. I grabbed my jacket, granola bar, and a bottle of water I had purchased at the gas station and followed Josh to his car.

He drove us to a neighborhood and turned down one of the streets. My mouth dropped open as I looked out the front seat passenger window. The houses were the largest I had ever seen. Their yards were meticulously manicured with cut lawns, landscaping, and trimmed bushes. He stopped the car.

"Here's your stop, Jess. I'll be back at sundown."

"What time is that?" I opened the passenger door.

"I'm guessing around six, seven, or maybe later. Just go to our pick-up point at dusk and wait."

I watched as he drove away to drop off the other two girls.

The morning air was chilly. I rubbed my hands together to warm them. Silly me, why did I think

Tennessee weather would be as warm as Florida. Dressed in a thin, sleeveless shirt, shorts, and flip-flops, I slipped on my jacket and zipped it up.

I looked at the impressive home nearest to me and exhaled. I thought of Heather and wished with all my heart that I was home. Until I could get there, I was determined to make as much money as I could.

I marched up the sidewalk and rang the doorbell. A well-dressed woman answered.

"Good morning. I am here to offer you the opportunity to save money." What did I just say? She did not need to save money. She looked quite wealthy. "For twenty dollars, I have a sheet of coupons you may use at nearby establishments." I held up the coupon sheet for her to see.

She reached out her hand while putting on her reading glasses hanging from a beaded necklace around her neck and scanned them. "Why yes, I go to several of these stores. You said twenty dollars?"

"Yes, mam."

"Just a moment." She disappeared, leaving the elaborate wooden door open, so I could peek inside of her house at the lovely foyer and winding staircase. Its beauty took my breath away. She returned and handed me a twenty-dollar bill in exchange for the coupons.

"Thank you. Have a nice day."

## A VICTIM OF DESPERATION

"You as well, my dear." She closed the door as I turned away.

With my confidence renewed, I crossed the yard onto the driveway on my way to the next house, stopped, and stared down at it. I had seen driveways made of grass, gravel, crushed limestone, asphalt, and cement. I had never seen one made of crushed seashells before. Was I close to the ocean?

I followed my map throughout the day, took time to eat my snack and drink for lunch, and sold all but three coupons. With my spirits lifted and dusk announcing the end of the day, I headed toward the pick-up point to meet Josh.

As he pulled up and stopped, I got into the front seat, and he handed me a bag.

"Here, I knew you missed out on breakfast, and I thought you may be hungry."

I opened the bag to see a cheeseburger and fries. Josh lifted a chocolate shake from the cupholder and gave it to me as well. I grinned as I took the shake and took the straw out of the bag.

"Thanks, Josh. That's very thoughtful of you." Even though the granola bar and water had gotten me through the day, it had been seven hours since I had eaten. I insisted on sharing the fries with him as we scarfed down the food and threw away the trash in a garbage can on a street corner before picking up the other girls.

Returning to the apartment complex, I inhaled the aroma of pizza as I entered the living room. Sam sat at a card table in the dining room, accepting returns. We turned in our collected money and unsold coupons. I rang the bell, and everyone applauded my achievement while Sam counted my unsold coupons, cash and scribbled the receipt.

"Well done, Jess. Let's hope you can sell all of your coupons tomorrow." He gave me the note and my commission for the day.

"Thank you." I stepped away and looked down at my receipt before counting my money and stopped dead in my tracks as I read it. Food? One day's rent? Gas? Are you kidding me? I did not get breakfast and gave Josh money for gas on the way here. I turned to argue, but Sam was reprimanding one of the girls who rode with us. I looked at the money in my hand. It was a twenty-dollar bill. I turned to Josh, who emerged from the kitchen with three slices of pizza on a paper plate and a can of soda. The carefree expression on his face faded as he perceived my disappointment and anger. He jerked his head to one side for me to follow him into the kitchen out of earshot of Sam.

## A VICTIM OF DESPERATION

I spat out what was on my mind through my clenched teeth. "What the hell is this?" I held up the unprofessional note and waved it in his face.

Josh snapped it from my hand, read it, and remained silent while he chewed his mouthful of pizza.

"Food?" I crossed my arms over my chest. "I had a half-glass of juice. I probably won't eat any pizza since we ate in the car."

"He charged you for it, so you might as well eat some."

"And gas? I gave you money to pay for gas on our way here."

Josh set his pizza on the counter, handed me the receipt, and reached into his back pocket, retrieving his wallet. He returned my seven dollars, which I gladly accepted.

He continued to eat after returning his wallet in its pocket. "You better grab a few pieces of pizza while you can." He motioned with the slice in his hand toward the quickly emptying boxes.

I grabbed a paper plate, loaded it with two slices, and turned back to him. "Rent?"

"Well, yes. This place isn't free, and you are staying here."

"It is a pigsty." I closed the distance between us until our noses were nearly touching. I could feel my blood pressure rising as my heart hammered in my chest. "I want to go home."

"Jess, I'm assigned here too. I can't leave either."

"There isn't even a phone here for me to call home and check on my daughter."

"It would be deducted from your daily sales if there was one." He reasoned.

"How am I supposed to know she is fine, that she is being cared for properly?"

"You left her with people you can trust, right?"

I thought of my aunt. I could count on her to care for Heather. Danny was questionable. I knew he was spending time at the local bars at night and dumping her off on Kathy. My neighbor is dependable and always took good care of my baby girl. I nodded my head reluctantly, indicating I had.

"Then there is nothing you should be worried about."

I turned away, grabbed a soda from the table, and sat in the corner next to my duffle bag. I looked at one of the girls from our car. She sat with her knees drawn into her chest, her arms wrapped tightly around them. She was not eating.

"There are pizzas in the kitchen. You better get a piece before it is all gone." I took a bite of one of the pieces from my plate.

## A VICTIM OF DESPERATION

She looked at my plate before her watery, bloodshot eyes met mine. "I'm not allowed to have any. By the time my rent, breakfast, and gas were deducted, I didn't have enough sales to pay for any pizza. I'm in debt and have to sell a lot of coupons tomorrow, or I will become further in debt and won't get to eat again."

I exhaled, disgust by the stupid policy. Is that what this game was about? Keep the workers in debt, so they had to remain in this hellhole forever. Maybe she would be moved to another city. Had she eaten breakfast? I pushed my plate with the remaining slice of pizza toward her. "I grabbed a snack earlier before we picked you up, so I'm not very hungry." I gave her my soda, knowing I still had some water in my bottle, which I could refill from the kitchen tap if necessary. I forced myself to eat the piece of pizza. After all, I paid for it. I paid for breakfast, too, even though I received little. I vowed to go directly to the kitchen upon rising tomorrow to guarantee I would get my money's worth in whatever they served.

The gal next to me reached for the pizza, paused, and looked at Sam's back, sitting at the table in front of us. She scooted on her butt, so her back faced him, timidly picked up the piece of pizza, and took a bite.

I glanced around the room. It was void of a TV, books, and even board games for entertainment. Many of the affiliates appeared tired after putting in close to ten hours of walking the streets. Conversations were kept to a decibel above a whisper. I watched as Josh folded the table and chair and followed Sam, who carried the cashbox to his bedroom.

Josh emerged from the hallway and plopped down on the carpet next to me.

In need of a shower, I looked at him. "Is there a clean towel I can use to take a shower?"

He looked at me and nodded. "Yes, under the sink. I wash the soiled ones during the day while you are going door to door. Just put your towel in the hamper when you are done."

So, there was a washer and dryer somewhere in the building. I had enough clothes with me to last a week or so before I needed to do laundry. I shuffled through my bag, grabbing my toiletries. I pulled out my pajamas, returned them, opting for a change in clothes instead, and went to the unoccupied bathroom.

There was a stack of clean towels under the sink as promised. I pulled back the shower curtain, cringed, and decided to wear my flip-flops while I bathed. I did not find a bar of soap on any of the four fiberglass molded shelves. I opened the medicine cabinet to see two boxes of soap neatly stacked. I ripped open a box, placed it on the edge of the tub, and turned on the water, hot enough to ease the tension in my body.

After combing my freshly washed hair and brushing my teeth, the steamy, misty cloud billowed out of the open door of the bathroom as I exited and returned to my claimed position on the floor. I thought of Heather, of Danny, as I returned my things to my bag and sat on the floor against the wall. Was anyone at home concerned, worried? They had not heard from me since I left.

Josh looked at me. "What are you thinking?"

His question pulled me from my thoughts. I looked at him, unsmiling. "I want to go home." I turned away from him as I lay on the floor, pulled my jacket over me, and closed my eyes.

# Another Day, Another Dollar

My eyes instinctively opened at the sound of the apartment door clicking shut. I blamed my motherly instinct on waking readily at the sound of Heather stirring in her bed. I looked to where Josh laid for the night. His place was vacant. Had he left for home without me? I sat up and scanned the room.

Even though people were crowded together while they slept, there was a chill in the air. The heat in the apartment must be off. Did they keep it off to save money? I slipped on my jacket over my short-sleeved shirt and rubbed my exposed legs to warm them, wishing I had packed jeans instead of shorts and capris.

## A VICTIM OF DESPERATION

Tiptoeing between those still asleep, I managed to make it to the bathroom without waking anyone and closed the door as quietly as I was able. My body jerked, startled by Sam's booming voice as he woke everyone. I used the bathroom and tried to rid myself of my bedhead hair before opening the door to see a line of people waiting for their turn.

Sam exited his room with an armload of coupon sheets and bumped into me before I could get out of his way. I hit the doorframe with my shoulder, quite positive it would bruise.

"Oops, watch yourself." He walked to the other side of the room without giving the mishap another thought.

I went to the kitchen hoping for bagels with cream cheese, breakfast sandwiches, or pancakes with maple syrup, but the counters and table were empty. No breakfast? My stomach grumbled.

The apartment door opened. Josh entered carrying boxes of donuts and a bag, which contained containers of juice. I unpacked the paper bag he set on the counter while he opened the boxes of donuts and retrieved napkins and paper cups from a cupboard. I grabbed a napkin from the stack and took two donuts. Pausing, I took a third donut and extra napkins. I lifted two paper cups from the stack, leaving them inside each other while I filled the top cup with juice.

I went to my corner and sat. As I bit into one of the donuts, a stack of coupons was waved before my face. I looked up to see Sam grinning. Was he trying to be funny? I grabbed the stack, sarcastically dropped them on the floor next to me, and stared at his back as he walked away.

The girl I shared my pizza with last night had yet to rise.

I leaned toward her. "I wasn't sure if you were allowed breakfast this morning, so I grabbed you a donut." I separated the paper cups, dumped half of my juice in the empty cup, and handed it to her before setting a napkin with the second donut next to her and nodded.

"Thanks." She sat up. "By the way, I'm Kendra."

"I'm Jessica, but just call me Jess."

"Who doesn't have their coupons for today." Sam bellowed as he held up a pack of twenty in his hand. Kendra placed her drink and donut behind her back before raising her hand, and Sam held a stack before her to accept.

"Ok, let's get started." He turned and went to the opening of the hallway to view the entire room, subtly hinting for us to listen and cheer when the time came. I took the third donut, wrapped it in a napkin, and slipped it into my jacket pocket.

After a not so motivating speech by Sam, I filled my water bottle in the kitchen on my way out the door to Josh's car.

I sat in the front seat, rubbing the gooseflesh on my legs. Josh gave us our maps and kindly flipped on the heat as he pulled out of the parking lot.

"Why didn't you bring warmer clothes?" He glanced at me.

"I have never been out of state before and thought the weather would be similar to what it is in Florida."

He dropped off the other two girls before turning the car into another affluent neighborhood and shifted the car into park. "See you at dusk."

My teeth chattered, and my toes became numb as I walked from house to house in my flip-flops. Even though I was determined to sell all my coupons, I soon discovered this neighborhood was less generous than the previous one.

The donut and water I packed were enough to get me through the day, but as the streetlights flickered on and I walked toward my pick-up point, my stomach grumbled. Josh was waiting for me as I turned the corner and hurried to his car.

"Any luck?" He looked at me as I sat in the front seat.

"Not like yesterday. I only sold five."

Kendra and the other girl did worse than I did. When the pizza was served for dinner, none of us were able to eat. We sat and watched those who exceeded their expenses enjoy their meal.

"Jessica."

I looked toward the hallway to see Sam.

"I need to speak to you." He turned and went into his bedroom.

I glanced at Josh, Kendra, and several others in the room, who stared at me as I rose and did as requested. I wrinkled my nose as my keen sense of smell detected the rancid stench of body oil and dirty clothes, causing me to pause at the bedroom doorway, hesitant to enter. In one corner, a pyramid of stacked boxes nearly touched the ceiling. One box, with its side torn away, revealed it contained coupon sheets. Against the opposite wall was a blow-up mattress. A single lamp on an overturned plastic crate next to his disheveled bed of twisted blankets and sheets illuminated the small room. Amber stains on his pillow and fitted sheet indicated where his body lay while he slept. A sheet covered the only window.

## A VICTIM OF DESPERATION

Sam sat down on the edge of the bed and patted the mattress next to him. "Have a seat."

An uneasy feeling caused the hair on the back of my neck to rise. I sat at the far end of the bed, as far away from Sam as I could get.

He scooted a little closer to me, but not close enough to touch me. I resisted the urge to rise from the bed. My heart pounded in my chest, and I tried to control my breathing. If he came any closer, I planned to bolt from the room.

"I just wanted to let you know that you can sleep in here with me instead of sleeping on the floor with everyone else." He displayed his crooked teeth when he smiled.

I held my breath, unable to believe my ears. Did I hear Sam correctly? Was this his way of asking me to have sex with him? I looked at his large hands, dirt beneath his untrimmed fingernails, and imagined them pawing at my naked body. My skin crawled, and I exhaled to calm myself. I learned long ago to pay attention to my body, my conscious, or perhaps my guardian angel. I had no intention of sleeping with him, not now, not ever.

I chose my words wisely. "I appreciate the offer, but it wouldn't be fair to the others who have to sleep on the floor." I rose from the bed and waited for his reply.

His smile disappeared as his face twisted and turned scarlet. "You fucking whore! You're nothing but a worthless, teasing bitch!" He stood from the bed as I inched my way closer to the doorway. "You worthless piece of shit! You are never going to amount to anything! Loser! You will always be a loser! Get out of here and don't come back in this room again!"

I have never been able to tolerate anyone yelling at me, mostly when it was unwarranted. Sam did not have to tell me twice. My eyes pooled with tears as I fled the room.

Everyone was staring at me as I entered the living room. Did they think Sam's accusations were true? I was sure my face was crimson as the heat rose in my cheeks. I went to my corner like a punished child ignoring everyone's prying, inquisitive stares. Sliding down the wall, I sat, pulled my knees toward my chest, and wrapped my arms around my knees to stop my legs from falling to the floor. Bowing my head, I touched my forehead to my knees and let my tears fall. I thought of Heather. I wanted to hold her in my arms and cuddle her against my chest. I thought of Danny and going home as murmured conversations floated around the room, assuming their topic of discussion was my encounter with Sam.

Someone grasped my shoulder.

## A VICTIM OF DESPERATION

"Don't cry." Josh consoled as he sat beside me. "Sam has tried to get nearly every girl in this room into his bed. I'm glad you refused."

"You could have warned me." I looked over my shoulder to see him staring at me. I wiped the dampness from my cheek. "I want to go home."

"I can't take you. I'm assigned here just like you. We just have to make the best of it for now."

The next morning, I avoided eye contact with Sam as he dropped coupons on the floor before me. Defiant, I helped myself to four donuts and juice, whether I was entitled to it or not. I was not going to starve, and, as far as I was concerned, neither were the two girls who pooled with me in Josh's car. We were being charged for breakfast anyway.

My days were beginning to blur together. I had worked every day since arriving at this godforsaken place. What day was it anyway? I missed my baby girl. I wanted to hold her in my arms, smell her baby shampoo hair, and watch her learn while she played. I wish I could call Danny, talk to him, and tell him I missed him.

Josh drove me to a different neighborhood. The street, littered with paper, and the trashcans looked as if they had been at the curb for several weeks. The houses reminded me of the territory I had worked closer to home, rundown and unkempt. With little hope in my heart for a successful day, I went to my first house and knocked on the door. I did my best to present my sales pitch while minimizing the chattering of my teeth.

At day's end, I looked at the map, hoping I was at the right corner. It was getting quite dark, and there were no streetlights. Maybe Josh was running late. I leaned against a trashcan and waited.

After a quick count of my unsold coupon sheets, I had sold only four. I wanted to give up and go home to Heather and Danny. Training? It was becoming apparent I would not receive the additional training they had offered. They had lied to me, made me feel as if it was my fault for being unable to sell my daily quota. If I could go home and return to working a territory, and not have to pay for the additional expenses they deducted from my sales. I could return to the restaurant too. I was confident I could sell my daily quota if I pushed myself a little harder.

Closing my eyes, I imagined holding a check made out for five hundred dollars in my hand, an amount that would come close to paying off my bills, which continued to accumulate while I was away.

"Hey, are you sleeping or what? Get in."

I opened my eyes to see Josh in his car with the passenger window down, staring at me. I climbed into the front seat and got right to the point. "Josh, I want to go home."

He stared at me before putting the car into drive. "Sorry Jess, as I have said, I'm required to be here for several weeks so, I'm unable to take you home."

"What about on Sunday when we aren't working?"

"Didn't Mrs. Smith tell you? We work seven days a week. In case you have lost track of time, you have already worked a Sunday."

I persisted. "I need to call home and check on my daughter."

He sighed. "I'm not supposed to allow you to use my cell, but if it eases your mind, I will go against protocol this once." He reached into the inside top pocket of his jacket and handed me his phone.

I stared at it in my hand, dumbfounded.

He glanced at me. "What's wrong?"

"I don't own a cell phone, so I don't know how to use one," I confessed.

He talked me through the task of dialing home.

I listened as my landline rang. More than likely, Danny had dumped Heather off on Kathy and was at the bar. "No answer." I handed the phone back. "Thank you."

Josh pushed a button before slipping the phone into his pocket.

# Catching A Break

Over the next week, I recognized a familiar pattern. We were assigned affluent neighborhoods for four days, maybe Monday through Thursday, and more impoverished communities on the weekend. Perhaps Sam realized, as I had when weekly paychecks were received, and people had the money to purchase coupons.

Each November day grew colder. I looked out the apartment window into the darkness at the well-lit parking lot. Was sleet blowing in the wind? I had noticed several houses along my daily route were beginning to decorate for Christmas. Automatic timers turned on their colorful lights at dusk. I wondered if I would be home for Thanksgiving or even for Christmas. My heart was heavy, aching for home.

The next day, I was dropped off in a nice neighborhood. At least I thought it looked pleasant by the condition of the houses. I had gotten in the habit of wearing two shirts under my jacket and my dirty pair of capris to stave off the biting cold. Kendra let me borrow a pair of socks, which looked silly wearing them with my flip-flops, but I did not care.

I sold twelve coupon sheets and hoped to make it thirteen as I walked up the sidewalk to a quaint bungalow. Neat and tiny, it resembled a residence of a little old lady. I knocked on the door, hoping to stop my teeth from chattering, so I could speak.

As anticipated, a well-dressed woman, I estimated her age to be seventy or more, answered the door.

I began my pitch, but she interrupted me.

"Honey, you look like you are freezing to death. Please, come inside." She opened the door wide enough for me to enter.

I knew it was against the rules to enter a house, but I was so cold, I did so anyway. "Thank you." I stepped into her tiny foyer and waited as she shut the front door.

## A VICTIM OF DESPERATION

"Come with me." She led me to the kitchen, where she had me sit on a chair at the table. "I'll just put on some water to boil for tea, or would you prefer a cup of coffee. I could make a pot for you."

I had covered a lot of the territory, and the warmth of the room was welcoming. I could afford the time for a simple cup of tea. "That is so kind of you. Tea would be nice." What did I care if I did not visit every house on my assigned route?

She took two homemade cookies from a tin she had on the counter, placed them on a saucer, and set them on the table. "Let me go turn off the TV. Other than Leo for company, I like to have it on for the noise. It gets too quiet in this house."

As she exited the room, an enormous tabby cat lumbered through the doorway. It was the largest feline I had ever seen. Its fur was long, and it had a bushy tail like a squirrel. I heard the TV go silent. "What kind of a cat is this? He looks like a mini-lion."

She smiled as she entered the room. "That's Leo. He is a Maine Coon. He is almost too heavy for me to pick up anymore. He weighed over thirty pounds the last time he went to the vet. I try and limit his food, but he gets cranky when I do."

The kettle began to whistle. The woman poured hot water into two teacups with teabags and carried them by their saucer to the table. She retrieved the sugar bowl, two spoons, and the carton of milk from the refrigerator before placing them on the table and sitting opposite me.

"Oh, I have forgotten my manners. I guess it happens when you live alone." She picked up the saucer of cookies and held it before me. "My name is Agnes."

I helped myself to a cookie, set it next to my teacup on the saucer, and boldly broke another rule. "I'm Jessica."

"It's nice to meet you, Jessica." Her voice was calming and grandmotherly soothing. "So, what are you doing out in this cold while being underdressed?"

"Selling coupons." I placed the remaining unsold eight on the table. I watched as she lifted the teabag by the string, scooped it with the teaspoon, held it over her cup, and used the paper tab to press out the excess water.

She smiled, almost studying my face as she added sugar and milk and used her teaspoon to stir her tea. "Something tells me there is more to your story than selling coupons." She brought the teacup to her lips, sipped while staring through her glasses at me. Her gray eyes projected kindness and compassion while she studied my face.

## A VICTIM OF DESPERATION

I sighed. "You won't believe me if I tell you." I squished my teabag against my spoon and added some sugar to my cup before stirring.

"I have all day to listen unless the good Lord decided to take me this very minute."

I smiled before sharing my tale of meeting Jim, my pregnancy, Heather, living in an apartment with my boyfriend, working three jobs, and my inability to make enough money to pay my bills. I explained how I answered an ad in the newspaper, went to the interview, and got my current job. I described the house office, being driven to each sales territory, and reduced commission after deducting the gas expense. I explained how I was coerced into coming to Tennessee, living in an unfurnished apartment with fifteen to twenty people, and having little to show for income after deducting the expenses.

"Bottom line, I just want to go home. I want to see my daughter, boyfriend, and family."

Agnes sat back in her chair. "My, that is quite some story. Have you asked to be taken home?"

"Yes, every day since I arrived."

"And they won't take you?"

"No. There isn't a phone in the apartment for me to call home. My leader let me use his cellphone once to call and check on my daughter, but my boyfriend was not home, so I don't know if she is OK or not."

"Do your parents know where you are?"

"No."

"Well, we can easily fix that. Reach behind you for the phone on the wall and call them."

I looked behind me to the phone above my head; its long cord twirled in a spiral. I looked back at Agnes. "It's a long-distance phone call. I don't have money to pay you for the expense."

"Just call." She left the room while I dialed my dad. The phone rang several times before he picked up.

"Hello."

"Hi, Dad."

"Jess, where are you?" Panic registered in his voice.

"That's a good question. I'm somewhere in Tennessee. I want to come home. How is Heather?"

"She is fine. Between your aunt, me, Danny, and your neighbor, we have been taking good care of her."

"I would have called earlier, but the apartment I am staying in doesn't have a phone."

"I take it you're not at the apartment then?"

"No, I was dropped off in a neighborhood to sell coupons, and a woman let me into her house to get warm and insisted I call you."

## A VICTIM OF DESPERATION

"Does anyone at the apartment have a cellphone you can use?"

I thought of Josh. "My leader does. He broke the rule once and allowed me to use it to check on Heather, but there was no answer at my apartment."

Dad was silent for a moment. "So, here's the plan. Ask him to use the cellphone to check on her. If he gives you a hard time, work yourself up to where you are crying. Once you convince him, call me and hand the phone to him. Tell him Heather wants to say 'hello.'"

"OK." I looked at the doorway as Agnes walked in, carrying a pair of shoes and a coat. "I have to go. Love you, Dad. Bye." I hung up the phone.

"I hope your feet are about the same size as mine. I know the coat isn't the latest style, but it should keep you warm." She held up the items for me to inspect.

I slipped on a pair of black ankle boots. They were a little large but fit well enough. Agnes held out the coat, and I pushed each arm through the sleeve as she lifted it onto my shoulders. I faced her as she buttoned the front closed. "There. That should get you by."

My eyes became misty. "Agnes, you are an angel. I appreciate your kindness in more ways than you can imagine. Thank you so very much."

"You are welcome, my dear. I just hope you get home."

"Me too."

She put several cookies in a plastic sandwich bag and gave them to me as we walked to the door together.

"Good luck, Jessica."

I turned around on the sidewalk to see her waving in the doorway. "Thank you, Agnes." I waved farewell.

I looked at the map on top of the remaining coupons for my rendezvous point. As I headed toward the designated intersection, I imagined several scenarios and came up with a viable excuse for my dated clothing.

Josh had yet to arrive. I calmed myself. I looked at the dated boots and aged detail of the coat, thanking God for Agnes.

Josh pulled up, and I got into the front seat.

"Good lord, where did you get that get up?" He scanned my attire.

"I found it on a porch in a bag for charity. It may be old, but it keeps me warm."

"Did you have a productive day?"

"I sold twelve."

"Not bad."

## A VICTIM OF DESPERATION

After picking up Kendra and the other girl, we headed back to the apartment, turned in our unsold coupons, received our pay, and ate pizza, again.

As everyone was settling down for the evening, I leaned toward Josh. "Can I talk to you in the hallway?"

He nodded and followed me out of the apartment door.

I took a deep breath and turned toward him as he closed the door, giving us some privacy. "I have been here for nearly two weeks. I need to call home and check on my daughter." I disliked deceiving him, but my pleas to return home had so far been ignored. I hoped my request was convincing as I tried to appear as if I was tearing up, and my bottom lip quivered.

He handed me his cell phone. I remembered the sequence of buttons I needed to press, held the phone to my ear, and waited for Dad to answer.

"Hello."

"Ah, finally, I've been able to get a hold of you. Is Heather, OK?"

"Is your leader next to you?"

"Yes."

"Tell him your daughter wants to say hello and hand him the phone."

My heart pounded in my chest. I lifted the phone from my ear and put a fake smile on my face. "My daughter wants to say 'hello' to you."

He exhaled and looked to the ceiling as he leaned against the wall, accepted the phone, and put it to his ear.

"Hello." I watched as his posture straightened, no longer needing the support of the wall. His eyes enlarged. He stared at me as if he were Julius Caesar, and I had just stabbed him in the back. He pressed a button to end the call and looked at me as he put his phone in his pocket. "I have to talk to Sam. Get your things and come back here."

I went to my corner, shoved my wayward clothes inside the bag, and zipped it shut. I looked at Kendra, who was watching me. I sat, took off the socks, and gave them to her. "Thank you."

"Are you leaving?"

"Yes, I managed to call my Dad. I don't know what he said to Josh, but he told me to gather my stuff. I am going home tonight."

She nodded. "I'm happy for you. Best of luck."

"Thanks, bye." I lifted the strap of my duffle bag to my shoulder and darted toward the door. As I grabbed the knob, I looked back at Kendra and glanced at the others in the room. What would happen to them? Will they ever return home? I lifted my chin, knowing I had to focus on myself. I went into the hall, slipped on Agnes's coat, and headed toward the apartment building door. I heard a door slam shut and heavy footsteps behind me. I hoped it was Josh and not Sam as I continued to the stairwell and the door to freedom.

"Well played, Jess."

I breathed a sigh of relief hearing Josh's voice behind me, pushed open the door, and stepped into the lit parking lot. "I did what I had to do. I need to get home to my daughter."

I threw my bag into the backseat of his car and sat in the passenger seat. I reached into the pocket of my capris pants, pulling out the three twenty dollar bills I had earned during my two weeks. I held one toward Josh. "To help pay for gas."

He glanced at me as he started the car and took the bill from my hand. "Thanks."

We did not talk much as he drove and only stopped for gas when necessary. Just past one in the morning, I saw Josh's head begin to bob from lack of sleep. I was too excited to close my eyes. I was familiar with the expressway we were on and quite confident it would take me to the largest city close to home. I knew my way from there.

"Why don't you pull over and let me drive? I'm not the least bit tired."

He sighed. "Sounds good to me. I'll get off at the next exit. We can fill up and switch places."

I took the opportunity to use the restroom and purchase a mocha coffee to help keep me awake, though I doubted I would need it. Once back on the road, Josh was soon asleep in the passenger seat with his head propped against the window.

My mind drifted to my reunion with Heather and Danny. A smile subconsciously extended across my face. I could plan a Thanksgiving dinner with my family, begin putting up what few Christmas decorations I owned, and make a list of presents I hoped to buy Heather to make her holiday special. My smile faded. How would I pay for the gifts? I was two months behind on my bills. The only option that came to mind was to continue selling coupons near my home, reducing the gas expense. I would insist on the territories of affluent neighborhoods. I could return to work at the restaurant, but the pay and tips were low and not worth my time. I would not ask Kathy for my babysitting job back. It did not seem right. I sighed. I would figure it all out once I got home.

I drove for several hours before the sky changed colors from midnight blue to pink, then orange, and the sun rose over the horizon. I pulled into my apartment complex parking lot and put the car in park in front of the main entrance.

Josh woke, lifting his head and looking about. "Where are we?"

"My apartment. Will you be returning to Tennessee right away?"

"No, I'll be at the house office for the week."

"Good. I want to come and talk to you tomorrow." I got out of the car, grabbed my bag, and went to the front door as he drove away. "Damn." My keys were inside the apartment. I was locked out. It was early, too early for Danny to be awake, but I had no other way of getting inside. I was about to press the buzzer to my apartment when someone, dressed nicely for work, opened the door as they left the building, and I scooted in behind them. I climbed the stairs, hurried to my apartment, and knocked on the door. No answer. Was Danny home? What day was it? Monday? Wednesday? I knocked again. Nothing, I pounded harder, no longer concerned about waking anyone in the adjoining apartments.

Danny opened the door dressed in his underwear.

"Jesus Chr...Jess. What the hell?"

"I'm glad to see you too." I was not in the mood to deal with his whining. I looked at the window across the room; colorful Christmas lights blinked off and on. I set my bag on the floor, went to Heather's crib, and stared at her angelic face. I wanted to pick her up, hold her to my chest, and kiss her brow, but I did not want to wake her. Our reunion could wait.

Danny wrapped his arms around my waist and whispered. "See, Heather is fine."

"I had to see for myself. I missed her." I turned to face him and wrapped my arms around his neck. "And I missed you."

He lowered his lips to mine and kissed me. "Are you home for good, or do you have to leave again?"

"I'm home, and right now, I am tired. We drove through the night."

"We?"

"Josh, my leader. I'll tell you about it after I get some sleep."

# Perseverance

I slept soundly and longer than I had intended. Stretching, I blindly reached my hand toward Danny's side of the bed. It was vacant, forcing my eyes to open and verify its emptiness. Had he taken Heather to my aunt's house? Wiping the sleep from my eyes, a child's giggle echoed from the living room, or was I so tired I imagined it? I smiled. It was good to be home again. I could see overcast skies through the sheer curtain of the window. They appeared gray and dotted with snow clouds, heavy with moisture. I sighed as I pulled the covers back and swung my legs to the carpeted floor.

My alarm clock indicated it was midmorning. I had slept for three hours, maybe four.

My daughter sat on the floor, playing with her toys. Dad watched her from the sofa with a drive-through cup of coffee in his hand. He smiled, clearly entertained by her antics. I stood in the doorway and watched, thankful to be reunited with both.

Aware of my presence, Dad looked at me. "Well, look who's awake." He set his coffee on the end table, rose, and gathered me into his strong, loving arms. "I'm glad you are at home." He kissed my forehead before releasing me.

"Me too."

"Mama." Heather dropped her toy and ran toward me with her arms held high.

"Hi, baby girl." I bearhugged her close to my body and covered her face with kisses. She placed her little hands on my cheeks to hold my head still and kissed me on the lips.

"So, do you want to fill me in on the details?" Dad returned to his seat and picked up his coffee.

I sat next to him with Heather on my lap and divulged my excursion's unpleasant experience.

Dad shook his head and rolled his lips inward. "You certainly got a lucky break with that woman who allowed you to call me. So, I suppose you will go back to the restaurant?"

"I thought about it while I drove home. Other than 'all you can eat night,' the job is a waste of my time."

"What's your plan then?"

"I have a little money left in my savings account. I will get another tax refund this year that will help get me by. However, that will be several months from now. I can call Mr. West, or at the very worst, stoop to the level of calling Jim's dad again." I sighed and pulled Heather's wispy blonde hair into a tiny ponytail. "I am very good at selling the coupons and managed to do well when I was assigned to an affluent neighborhood, so I thought I would go back and see if I can still work for them."

Dad's eyebrows drew together. "I don't think that is a good idea. It sounds to me as if they had you work for little to nothing while they reaped the benefit of your labor."

"I didn't make much money because I had to pay for rent, gas, and food while I was away. Now that I am home, I should be able to earn more."

"I disagree, but I can see you are determined to prove me wrong." He stood. "I have to get going." He outstretched his arms and embraced his granddaughter and me. "I'm glad you are back home." He planted a kiss on each of our cheeks.

"Me too, Dad." Heather tried to wiggle out of my arms, so I placed her on the floor. She returned to her toys as I walked him to the door. "Bye, and thanks." With a wave of his hand, he left.

I shut the door and took a deep breath as I leaned against it. It was good to be home again. However, I needed to talk to Josh and see if I could continue selling coupons. I took a quick shower, dressed, and dropped Heather off for a few hours at my aunt's house.

The house office appeared lifeless, vacant as I parked my van next to the curb. Josh's car was in the driveway, so I knew he was there. I entered the empty front room. Everyone was at their assigned territory selling coupons. The door to Mrs. Smith's office was cracked open, and I could see the back of Josh's head. He was talking to someone. I prayed it was not Mrs. Smith sitting behind her desk. I did not want to interrupt their conversation, but I was determined to know the truth. I knocked on the frame.

Josh spun around in the office chair and looked at the door. He was chatting on his cellphone and hung up. "Come in."

## A VICTIM OF DESPERATION

I entered to find him alone and watched as he stood and placed his cellphone in his pocket.

"Hi, Jess."

"I am at a crossroads, and I need a straight answer."

"OK." He went behind Mrs. Smith's desk and stood as I entered the room.

"I have bills to pay and must provide for myself and my daughter. I need to know if I am ever going to make money selling coupons, and if the five hundred dollar checks you showed me are even possible."

He pushed a few papers around on the table. Was he avoiding the question?

"Josh?"

He looked at me. "You need to find another job."

"Thank you for being honest." I walked out of the house, vowing never to return.

# Another Year Older

Danny was at work. Heather and I were just finishing mac and cheese for lunch when a knock sounded on my door. I thought it may be my neighbor but was surprised to open the door to see my father standing there with a birthday cake and a quart of ice cream in his hands.

"Dad! How did you get into the building?"

"I buzzed Kathy." He nodded his head in the direction of her apartment. "She let me in." He stepped through the door as I held it open and set the cake and ice cream on the kitchen table before kissing Heather on the top of her head. He sat in a chair as I resumed my seat. "I thought we would celebrate your birthday."

"That's very thoughtful of you." I finished the last few bites of my lunch. "There is still some mac and cheese left. Would you like some?"

"No, thanks. I ate before I came over." He picked up Heather's fork and helped her eat the last few bites of food on her tray. "How are you getting along?"

I looked over my shoulder as I set my dirty dishes in the sink. I retrieved two plates, forks, and a knife. "So far, so good. My savings account is slowly dwindling, but I have enough to get by, for now. I had to call Jim for child support. I'm quite certain his parents put up the money. With Danny chipping in to pay half of the bills, we should be fine. I just have to figure out what I want to do next."

Dad pulled a box of candles from his pocket. "Got a lighter?"

I opened the junk drawer, retrieved the one I used to light candles, and returned to my seat. Dad inserted a candle into the cake, lit it, and sang to me. Heather stared at him, fascinated, with a silly grin on her face. I made a wish and blew out the candle. Heather thought it was funny when my dad clapped, and she imitated him. I cut the cake and served everyone.

"Are you making your usual rounds for Thanksgiving?" Dad cut into his piece of cake with the side of his fork.

"Sure. It wouldn't be our normal Thanksgiving otherwise."

~

Our Christmas was pleasant. We visited each family, enjoyed good company, and ate delicious meals. Even though I only bought Heather a few small gifts and clothes, she received plenty of presents from other family members. I met Mom's boyfriend. He seemed rather nice and took a liking to Heather the moment he saw her.

With my holiday decorations packed away and the apartment looking rather bare, I watched Heather play with her new kitchen set while I folded a load of laundry. I looked out the window to see snow drifting down from the overcast sky. I wondered. Was it snowing in Tennessee? What happened to Kendra and the others? Were they selling tickets in the cold? I smiled. Thank God for angel Agnes. I kept her coat and shoes as a reminder of her kindness. I looked at the closet by the apartment door where they were stored.

"Mom, mom." Heather plopped a plate with a plastic banana on it next to me on the couch.

"Thank you. You are such a good cook, Heather." I picked up the next item in the basket and folded it.

I decided to make peanut butter and jelly sandwiches and chips for lunch and thought it would be fun to have an indoor picnic using Heather's dishes from her kitchen set. I spread one of her blankets on the floor, brought the cut sandwiches on a saucer from the kitchen, and her sippy cup containing milk.

"Heather, bring me two plates."

She held up a plate with a questioned look on her face.

"Yes, another one, please, and come here."

She handed the plates to me and watched as I put a quarter sandwich and chips on each.

"Sit down."

She did so, picked up her sandwich, took a healthy bite, and smiled. I wished I had a camera to capture the moment.

After a quick diaper change and placing Heather in her bed for a nap, I washed her dishes and returned them to her kitchen to resume play when she woke. The mail had arrived in the lobby. I was excited to discover my tax return forms inside my mailbox. My expected refund would help tide me over for a while longer until I could decide what to do. I retrieved old pay stubs and bills to be paid for the end of the month and set them on the table when a knock sounded on the door and answered it.

"Hi, Kathy. Come on in." I stepped aside for her to pass.

"I can't stay long. My little ones are asleep, so I thought this would be a good time to come and tell you something."

"Good timing. Heather is asleep too."

Kathy glanced around the apartment. "Is Danny here?" She entwined her fingers and wrung her hands as we sat on the couch.

"No, he's at work." My eyebrows drew together. My curiosity was piqued.

"Good." She exhaled and looked away from me.

"So, what do you need to tell me?"

She inhaled and sighed as if trying to work up enough courage to say what she must. "While you were away, Danny, um, had an affair, um, with the woman who lives in the apartment four doors down the hall." She was referring to the blonde bombshell that was known as common property by the building's residents.

My mouth dropped open. I held my breath momentarily, then exhaled. "Are you sure? I mean, I knew he was going out to the bar several times a week, but are you sure?"

## A VICTIM OF DESPERATION

Kathy shrugged her shoulders. "I saw him with her several times. I'm sure." She nodded her head slightly.

I sat stunned, hurt, and my anger began to boil like a slowly heating kettle of water.

Kathy reached out and put her hand on top of mine, resting in my lap. "I'm sorry. I know this is quite a shock, but in all fairness, I thought you should know."

I took a deep breath, stood, and began pacing the floor. "How long has Danny been seeing her?"

"I'm not quite certain. I think before you went away. I suspected something was going on when Danny kept having me watch Heather. I cracked the door open after he dropped her off once and watched as he went down the hallway and enter the woman's apartment."

My mind raced, trying to remember when he began going out several times a week. Wasn't it right after moving into the apartment? The veil over my eyes had been removed by the truth. He did not want to settle down and acted like a kid who refused to grow up, at least not yet, and not with me. I took a deep breath and faced Kathy. "Thanks, yes, I needed to know."

She stood. "I didn't want to see you being played the fool."

"Too late." I tried to smile even though I was on the verge of tears. "Thanks, and thanks for watching Heather every time he went out."

"Any time."

I walked Kathy to the door. She turned and hugged me before stepping into the hallway, and the door clicked shut.

I tried to come to terms with the heartbreaking news. Should I go and confront the woman down the hall? Would Danny tell me the truth if I confronted him with the accusation?

I had dinner on the table when he arrived home. I could hardly contain the burning questions within my mind, but I waited until we were done eating.

"Kathy stopped by today."

"Oh."

"Yes, she had some interesting news."

"Really?"

"Yes, she said while I was in Tennessee, you were having an affair with the woman down the hall. You know, the blonde slut."

He remained silent and would not look at me.

My eyebrows raised, and I crossed my arms over my chest as I waited for his reply.

"Sorry." He finally stated.

## A VICTIM OF DESPERATION

"Sorry? That's all you have to say for yourself. Sorry?" I tried to keep the volume of my voice low, as not to startle Heather, who continued to eat her meal in her highchair.

He took a sip of his beer and paused with it in his hand. "What do you want me to say? You were gone. I didn't know when you would be back."

"I expected you to be loyal, faithful. I was. I didn't cheat on you. From what I understand, you started cheating on me the moment you moved into the apartment, didn't you?"

"Yes, I know. You are a saint."

"No, I'm not a saint, but I am capable of making better choices." I rolled my lips inward. My trust in him was destroyed. "I think we are done. I need you to move out by the end of the month. I'll get some cardboard boxes and begin packing your stuff tomorrow."

"Why should I move out? I pay half of the rent."

"Fine, I'll move out."

"Jess." He reached across the table and tried to grab my hand, but I pulled it away before he could touch me.

"It's over." I picked up my dirty dishes and placed them in the kitchen sink.

# On My Own

Danny slept on the couch that night. He packed his things the next day and moved out of the apartment. On my own, I relied on my savings account and child support to get me through the last three months of my lease. My tax return was filed as early as possible, and I received my refund in February but knew the amount would only last a few months.

Searching through the want ads while at the library one Saturday morning, I found an advertisement for an available, less expensive apartment. I went directly to the complex office and requested an application from the manager. Even though I did not have a job, I put the amount I should be receiving for child support from Jim as income and made a sidenote of the balance in my savings account.

Much to my relief, my application was accepted, and I would move into my new residence on April Fool's Day. I got cardboard boxes from the grocery store. With a week to spare, I packed my things, eager to put the memories of this apartment behind me. I needed to find a job. Thank goodness my old van had held up so far, but I knew I was pushing my luck and would need a new vehicle soon.

My new one-bedroom apartment was only a few miles away. Heather and I went to the complex the day before moving in to pay for our first month's rent and take a tour. The laundry was conveniently located at the end of the hallway. I anticipated Heather's joy while playing in the swimming pool.

Kathy watched Heather on the day of my move. I carried boxes to my van, filled it, and drove to my new place of residency. With my first box in hand, I juggled the building key to unlock the outside door when it opened on its own, and I stared up into a guy's hazel eyes. He appeared to be my age. He smiled.

"Moving in?" He held the door open for me to pass.

"Yes, thank you."

"I'll put the wedge in the door, so you don't have to use your key every time. Just take it out when you are finished."

"Thanks," I called over my shoulder as I climbed the stairs to the second floor, unlocked my apartment door, and entered. Thankful I had labeled each box, I set this one in the kitchen to unpack later and went to retrieve the next box.

Dad was waiting outside the building of my old apartment when I returned for my furniture. With some effort on my part, we loaded my hand-me-down sofa, the end table, and a few lamps. He climbed into the front seat, and we were on our way.

My heartbeat increased, eager to show Dad my new apartment, or was it from the exertion of carrying the sofa to the van? I pulled into the parking lot.

"It looks nice, and you have a pool too." Dad scanned the building and area. "The landscaping looks well-kept."

The spring flowers were in bloom, and the shrubs, neatly trimmed. "I failed to notice, but now that you mention it, I agree." I nodded with pride as I looked at him.

I carried a lamp in each hand as Dad brought the end table into my new home.

"It's smaller than my other apartment, but I think it will be fine," I explained as Dad peeked into the only bedroom.

"It's perfect for the two of you." He agreed as we went to retrieve the sofa and stepped into the hallway.

I pointed to my right. "The laundry is at the end of the hallway. I'm thankful I don't have to go to the laundromat."

"Nice and convenient."

We struggled, well, I did, to take the sofa out of the van and carry it into the building.

"Here, let me help." Came a male voice from behind me as strong hands lifted the burden from my arms.

I looked at the guy, another about my age. He stared down at me with a nod and a smile.

"Thank you." Was divine intervention pushing itself into my life? Two handsome, strong gentlemen coming to my rescue when I needed them in the middle of the day. I was not looking for a relationship with anyone. After all, I needed to focus on myself and get a job. Didn't they have jobs?

I did not like the idea of him knowing where I lived, but his help was appreciated, nevertheless. I stood helplessly by as the sofa was lowered to the carpeted floor. "Thank you."

"You're welcome." He nodded. I noticed a backpack on his back as he exited the apartment.

Dad and I made several trips back and forth to transport the remainder of my furniture. On our last trip, I knocked on Kathy's door.

"Thanks, you have been a godsend and were always there when I needed you most." I embraced my friend, picked up Heather, and placed her on my hip.

"Any time. You know where to find me if you ever need someone to watch Heather."

"Thanks." The two of us left the building to begin anew.

Heather rode securely in her car seat in the van with me. Dad followed in his car. Once at the apartment, we unloaded the last few items.

"Well, that about does it." He brought in the mattress for the crib and set it in the bedroom. "I'll go get us something to eat. A sub perhaps?"

My stomach grumbled. "A sub sounds great."

"OK. Be right back."

Heather had reached the end of her patience. "Mama, up." She held her arms up, stuck her lower lip out, and was on the verge of crying.

I clapped my hands together in front of me and held my arms toward her. "In know, baby girl. You have been so good. Let me see if I can find you a snack for you to eat until Grandpa gets back." She pushed me away as I tried to snuggle her closely in my arms. She is such a 'Miss Independent' nowadays. I wonder where she gets that attitude from?

I moved the couch aside and pushed it against the wall, put an end table next to it, and set the lamp on top. After shifting several boxes, Heather had enough room to play, but she was more interested in her new surrounding and was off exploring the apartment.

First, I needed to put the legs on the kitchen table, so we had somewhere to eat lunch. The tabletop was easy to locate, but it took a while to search through the boxes to find the legs and bolts. Thank goodness I remembered to put the screwdriver in the plastic bag with the hardware. I could hear Heather chattering to herself as I tightened the first bolt. "Baby girl, what are you doing?"

Her vocabulary was limited, but I managed to understand a few of the babbles she spoke as she came out of the bedroom with a dolly she found.

"Baby." She held it before me.

"Oh, you found your baby. Good job." She turned and ran back to the bedroom. I flipped the table onto its legs and placed the four chairs around it as Dad entered the apartment and set our meal on the table. He retrieved the highchair while I unpacked the subs from the bag and inserted straws in our drinks.

"Heather, do you want to eat?" Her footsteps echoed from the hallway as she ran into the room. I lifted her into her chair and broke off several pieces of my sub for her to begin eating. I managed to find her sippy cup in a box and filled it with water before joining Dad at the table. I sighed as I sat, appreciating the moment to rest.

"Thanks, Dad, for all of your help and the food." I sunk my teeth into the soft bread of the sub.

Dad nodded and smiled as he chewed his food, forcing it down his throat, and took a sip of his soda. "You are welcome."

Heather would need a nap soon, so Dad and I assembled my bed and her crib after lunch. With her down for a nap, he helped me get the living room in order and hang a few pictures, mostly of Heather, on the wall before he left. I organized the kitchen before sitting on the couch and looked around the apartment. Even though my relationship with Danny ended and I lived alone for the past three months, it was nice to be surrounded by walls free of his memory. It was a new start, a new beginning. The question was, how was I going to survive. My tax money was running low, and I was in fear of not being able to pay my next month's rent.

## A VICTIM OF DESPERATION

I hoped to receive my security deposit from my old landlord soon. I needed to find a new job.

# The Stars Align

I soon learned the gentlemen who helped me moved into the apartment were a group of college guys who lived directly below me and liked to party late into the night with the bass turned up on their stereo. I had to admit, they had good taste in music. My bed vibrated to the beat as I tried to fall asleep during some of their wilder gatherings.

The guys were a friendly bunch, cute too. Whenever I saw one of them passing, they offered an invitation to attend one of their parties. I declined each one.

## A VICTIM OF DESPERATION

A guilty pang pierced my heart as I called Jim's dad and ask for child support money once again. Jim should accept the responsibility and provide for his daughter, not his dad.

As the month waned, the outside temperature was relatively warm. I took Heather on a walk to ease my mind and meandered toward the swimming pool. I opened the gate, scanned for a place for us to sit, and smiled as I saw a familiar face from the tanning salon.

She laid on a lounge chair. Her perfect bronze body soaking up the sun.

Carrying Heather on my hip, I sat on the lounge chair beside her and placed my daughter in my lap. "Hello, Candy. I didn't know you lived here?"

She opened her eyes, shielding them with her hand. Smiling, she sat up. "Jess, when did you move in?"

"Close to a month ago. I'm on the second floor. But I don't know how much longer I can stay. My money is tight." I didn't know why I was telling her about my financial worries. With only having Heather for company, I guess it was nice to speak to an adult. "Heather's father, Jim, doesn't pay child support regularly. In truth, he never pays it. Even though I hate doing so, I call his father when necessary, and he submits the money to the child support office. I should have the money in a few days." I could not contain my tears. All my worry, anxiety, and frustration were released as droplets cascaded down my cheeks. I was embarrassed, falling apart right in front of her. "I feel so guilty, asking Jim's father for money."

Candy swung her legs to the side of the lounger, sat up, and patted my knee. "Hey, what are all of the tears for?"

I wiped away the dampness from my cheeks. "You won't believe me if I tell you."

"Try me." She folded her hands in her lap and tilted her head to one side.

I sighed, trying to compose myself. I began to explain how I met Jim and ended my tale with moving into my new apartment. Did she think I was being responsible by providing for myself and my daughter, or did she think I had made stupid choices that resulted in the current mess I was in? I kissed the top of Heather's head before looking into Candy's eyes for her reaction to my tale of woe.

"Holy crap, girl. You're lucky you aren't dead. No wonder I haven't seen you at the tanning salon for quite some time."

"Anyway, I'm running out of money. If I pay my rent for May, I don't have any money for my bills or food."

"You can come and work with me."

## A VICTIM OF DESPERATION

My eyebrows raised, and my mouth fell agape. "Exotic dancing?" I glanced at her shapely legs, beautiful face, and ample bustline. "No, I can't even begin to compare to you. I'm not pretty enough, too short, and need to have my bra size grow about five inches."

"Jess, don't sell yourself short. You are as cute as a button."

I shook my head in disagreement as she went on.

"Trust me, you can make so much money dancing. I only work two, maybe three nights a week at most."

At her admission, my eyes nearly popped out of my head. Only two nights a week? Seriously? How many jobs had I worked over the years, putting in ungodly hours, wearing myself to the bone? I would need someone to watch Heather only two nights a week, a much lower babysitting bill than I paid in the past.

"Candy, I don't know if I have the guts to dance in front of a bunch of men."

"No worries, they can't touch you. Just stay away from the alcohol and drugs, and you will be raking in the dough."

I wrinkled my nose. "Do I have to dance naked?"

"We never dance totally naked. We wear lingerie while we dance. You know, the sexy stuff with a bra and panty or thong. We have a DJ, and he announces when we take our tops off. It's usually later in the evening, like eleven or twelve o'clock. You don't have to and can opt-out of your last dance shift or two, but that's when we make the most in tips. Probably because the men have gotten a few drinks in them by then. Chances are, you won't know anyone in the audience anyway, so who cares."

"I don't know." I smoothed Heather's hair pulling it back into a tiny ponytail, stalling for time to think.

"Get someone to watch your little one and come with me to work on Friday night. Be at my apartment at 6:00, so the girls and I can get you dressed and show you what to do. We work from 7 to 2. If it is a slow night, we can leave early. You get to keep all your tip money at the end of the night, but you must pay the bouncers, bartenders, and DJ. If you want a nice introduction by the DJ, give him a tip."

"How much do you normally pay them?"

"I usually give the DJ $30, but he charges $15, $10 to each bouncer, there is either one or two of them every night, and $15 to each bartender."

"How many bartenders are there?"

"Two to three. The guys make you pay upfront, so they don't get stiffed."

## A VICTIM OF DESPERATION

"I guess my rent will have to be late if I have to pay upfront."

"Pay your rent. I'll lend you the money. You can pay me back once you get your tips."

I stood placing Heather on my hip and looked at Candy, who pointed toward a patio with a sliding glass door where she lived.

"I live on the first floor, in the first apartment by the main entrance. Meet me at 6:00 Friday if you are interested."

"I'll think about it. Thanks." I left the pool wrestling with the morals of dancing half-naked in front of a bunch of men. Could I really make enough money to pay the DJ, bartenders, and bouncers each night and still have plenty of money to live on? I was tired of scrimping by and disliked calling Jim's dad for child support. I set Heather down as I entered our apartment. It was lunchtime, so I grabbed the tasteless loaf of bread, the peanut butter, and grape jelly. I opened the cupboard and grabbed a can of no-brand peaches I purchased from the dollar store.

"Perfect."

Heather and I split a sandwich and the can of peaches. With her down for a nap, I called my Dad.

"Hello." His comforting voice brought a calmness to my jittery insides.

"Hi, Dad."

He must have detected the indecisiveness in my voice. "What are you planning, or what do you need?"

Did I only call him when I needed something? I would have to make more of an effort to phone him just to chat. "I need your advice." I heard him exhale on the other end of the line.

"OK."

"I have exhausted nearly all of my tax money. Out of desperation, I called Jim's dad to ask for child support, but you know how that goes. His dad will pay for it instead of making Jim pay it himself."

"Yes, he's an enabler. If he were my son, I would have kicked ass to the curb years ago."

"I know. Anyway, when I worked at the tanning salon, many of the exotic dancers tanned there regularly. I got to know them pretty well."

"Where are you going with this, Jess?" The tone in his voice conveyed a forewarning.

"One of the dancers lives in my apartment building. I met her at the pool. When I started telling her about my financial situation, I started blubbering like an idiot. She has offered to get me into the place where she dances. What do you think?"

My question was met with silence. I could only imagine what was going through Dad's mind. I was raised in a rather strict Christian environment. Dancing in lingerie, or otherwise, in front of strangers was frowned upon.

"Will you be naked?"

"No. From what I understand, I will be wearing lingerie. From what Candy has…"

"Candy? Is that her real name?"

I laughed. "Actually, Dad, it is. She told me I can dance in lingerie and when the DJ announces for the dancers to take off their tops, I can leave the stage. But if I decide to take off my top, she said the tips flow like a green river onto the stage." I believe my attempt to justify my nudity failed as I heard only silence, no response. I waited for him to speak.

"I worry about your safety. Can the men touch you?"

"No, and there are several bouncers on duty for our protection."

"When do you work?"

"Friday. I am planning to call Aunt Angela to watch Heather."

"You won't be home until two or three in the morning, so she will have to stay all night at her house."

I had not thought of that. I guess it would give me time to get a few hours of sleep before picking Heather up in the morning. If I danced Friday and Saturday,

Heather would be shuffled back and forth for only two days a week, that is, if I continued to dance.

"Yes, unless she was with Jim for the weekend." I sighed. "I thought I would give it a try for one night. Who knows? I may not like it and not return Saturday. I mean, I don't plan to do this as a career. Just until I can get financially sound."

"Well, if that's what you want to do, I'll support you. I don't like the idea of my daughter flaunting her stuff but give it a try and see if it is worth your time."

"Thanks, Dad. I'll let you know how it goes."

"Bye, Honey."

"Bye." I sighed, a little relieved knowing Dad approved, well, kind of approved. I called my aunt and lined her up to watch Heather.

Once Heather woke from her nap, I would visit Candy and ask the questions that haunted my mind. Where would I get the lingerie? Would I have to wear a lot of make-up? A wig? What about shoes? Didn't exotic dancers wear stiletto heels? As short as I am, I should own at least one pair of stiletto heels, but I did not. I did not have a wig either or lingerie. God, what was I getting myself into?

I went to the bedroom and pulled the door partially closed to look at myself in the full-length mirror hanging on the back of the door. I was pretty. Some have described me as cute. But beautiful? No, not stunningly beautiful like Candy and the other girls who visited the tanning salon. I turned and looked at the profile of my body—unfortunately, not much of a bustline. My butt, I always thought it was a little too big. I nodded my head. "I think I can do it. I'm not certain about my ability to dance exotically, though." I whispered to myself and hoped Candy could give me a few pointers. Wait, did the dancing incorporate a pole?

# Taking The Stage

"You're pretty quiet." Candy kept her hands on the steering wheel as she drove us to work. "Are you scared? Having second thoughts?"

I had taken Heather to my aunt's house for the evening. I took a shower so that my hair was freshly washed and ensured my makeup was not whorishly too much. I took a deep breath and exhaled, hoping to calm my nerves. "Yes, petrified. I don't know if I can do this. I mean, I was raised in a conservative religious family."

"Just think of it as a job, a way to get some money and get back on your feet."

# A VICTIM OF DESPERATION

The 'place of business' was a short drive away. It was a good thing because if I had sat in the car much longer, I would have insisted Candy turn it around and take me back to my apartment.

We pulled into the parking lot. I stared at the building, unmoving.

"Are you ready?" She put the car in park and shut off the ignition before looking at me.

I looked at Candy, who was grinning. "Ready as I will ever be."

As we entered the establishment, Candy pulled a wad of dollar bills from her purse and peeled-off several, handing some to each bouncer, bartender, and DJ.

"Hey, Benny, this is Jessica. This is her first night. Can you give her a big intro and make her feel welcome?" She handed him an extra twenty-dollar bill.

"Sure thing, Candy." He looked at me. "Glad to have you with us, Jessica. Did you want to use a stage name?"

Stage name? I looked at Candy. "Do I?"

"Only if you want to."

My mind raced. What stage name would be appropriate? Bunny? Bambi? Kitten? Nothing popped into my mind except terms for animals. No, I did not want to sound too slutty. I looked at the DJ. "My real name is fine."

"You got it." He nodded his head before redirecting his attention to the table of equipment in front of him.

Candy disappeared behind a black curtain and held it open for me to follow. She led me through a short hallway and into a small room where other dancers were preparing for the evening. There were several dressing tables, each containing a large mirror framed with bright clear lightbulbs. The tabletops were littered with various make-up, perfumes, and bottles of hairspray. Several of the women, seated before them, turned and looked at me.

Candy motioned for me to stand beside her as she stood next to an empty dressing table. "Hey, everyone. This is Jessica. She will be joining us tonight, so let's make her feel welcome."

I fanned my fingers, giving a single wave, almost afraid to speak. "Hi."

A woman dressed in a pink fuzzy robe rose from her chair. Her eyes were dark blue like the midnight sky, and her long blonde hair the color of a bale of straw. She held out her hand.

"Hi, I'm Samantha, but my stage name is Athena, you know, like the goddess."

I shook her hand. "It's nice to meet you, Samantha."

She scanned up and down my body. "I think you are about my size. Let's see what we can find for you to wear." She grasped my hand. I looked back at Candy as I was led to a rack of clothes, if you could call them that. I scanned Samantha's body and had to agree; we were about the same size. She began shifting hangers of lingerie back and forth until she paused, thought for a moment, looked at me, and pulled the item from the rack. "This should do nicely." She held it before me and motioned with her hand like a model on a gameshow displaying an item.

I stared at the skimpy pink boa bra with a sheet cloth attached that would cover my abdomen. The panties matched the bra. Uncertain, I raised my eyebrows. "I've never worn anything like that in my life."

"Well, your life is about to change." She pushed the outfit into my hand. "Now, let's find you a pair of shoes to match. What size do you wear?"

"Six." I looked at Candy for reassurance.

She smiled. "Men like the pink outfit. It projects an innocence in those who wear it."

"An innocence?" I did not consider myself innocent. After all, I was a mother and have had two boyfriends in my life.

"Yes, you'll collect a lot of money wearing it." Candy nodded before turning to her mirror and pulling a blush brush from a canister on her desktop.

"Here you go."

I turned to see Samantha waving a pair of matching pink four-inch stilettos. My mouth dropped open. "I'm supposed to dance in those?"

"Sure. Just use the pole to keep your balance."

"Pole?" My worst nightmare had come true. Was I supposed to hump a pole all night?

"Unless you want to freestyle it?" She tilted her head to one side and waited for my reply.

I looked at the length of the heels as she handed them to me. "No, I have a feeling I will need it to keep me from falling on my face."

Candy paused from putting on eye make-up and pointed with her eyeliner pen toward an open doorway. "You can change in the bathroom."

I flicked on the light switch before shutting the door. "What have I gotten myself into?" I stared at my face in the mirror above the sink. "I'm doing this for Heather." I reminded myself as I exhaled, trying to relieve my anxiety.

I dressed in the skimpy outfit, quite thankful for the sheer material that made me feel partially covered. I looked in the mirror. "Not bad." I convinced myself. I slipped on the shoes and was surprised at how easy they were to walk in. "Maybe I can pull this off after all." I stared at myself in the mirror, thankful I did not have stretch marks from my pregnancy. "I don't really have any other choice, now do I?"

I joined the dancers in the room. Everyone looked at me as I entered, making me a little self-conscious. I pulled the pink boa at the bottom of the sheer cover-up trying to make it longer, if possible.

"You look great." Candy handed me a robe. "Here. Let's get your face on."

I placed my clothes on the top of her dressing table, slipped on the robe, sat in a chair before the mirror, and watched as she applied various make-up. I hoped she would not make me look too risqué. She pinned my hair away from my face and looked at my reflection in the mirror.

"I think that about does it. You look great." She took a hand mirror from the top of her dressing table and gave it to me.

I turned my head from side to side, looked in the hand mirror as I turned away to see the back of my head framed by the bright lights in the mirror. "I guess I clean up pretty well. Thank you, Candy."

"Follow me, and we will see what you can do on the pole."

We walked to the stage. Candy flipped on the overhead lights. I was thankful the black curtain was closed so no one could see how foolish I may look at my first attempt at dancing in stilettos.

"As you can see, there are several poles on stage. We dance for about an hour and switch out with the dancers who arrived late or decided to take the second-hour shift of the night."

"How many hours will I have to dance?"

"We start at seven and end at two. When you aren't dancing, you are to remain in the dressing room, for safety sake."

I nodded my head before she continued.

"Benny makes the announcement when we are to remove our tops. During the midnight and one o'clock shifts. The tips tend to increase, so it helps distribute them evenly between the two shifts."

"I can only imagine."

"You don't have to dance either of those shifts if you don't want to. Do it when you are comfortable."

"OK."

"Now, drop your robe, and let's see some of those dance moves."

I untied the belt and toss the robe aside.

"Benny will introduce you and start the music for you to begin dancing."

# A VICTIM OF DESPERATION

I looked at the pole, silently vowing not to grind against it. "I have never danced with or on a pole before, so how does someone normally do it?"

"Whatever you feel most comfortable doing or what you think the men would like to watch. Here is what I normally do." She grabbed the pole with one hand and began to gyrate her hips, sliding her backside down it until she was in a crouched position, and turned toward the pole while wiggling her hips to stand while sliding her leg up it until she extended her leg fully next to her head doing the splits.

My mouth dropped open. I snapped it shut. "I don't think I'm that flexible, but I should be able to entertain the audience. I just hope the men don't laugh."

"They don't expect you to be a gymnast. Remember, the bouncers are here for your protection, and the 'guests' are not allowed to touch you."

"Don't they stuff money in my underwear?"

"No, not in this establishment. They place it on the floor in the basket in front of you. You collect it at the end of your hour of dancing. Benny announces when your hour is up." Candy parted the curtain and looked at the audience. "We have a fairly good crowd already. You can go on first and dance the seven, nine, and eleven o'clock shifts. If you feel comfortable enough to take off your top, you can dance the one o'clock. If not, someone else can take your shift."

"OK."

"I am dancing for the same hours at the pole next to you." Candy clasped my upper arm. "You can do this."

I chuckled. "I don't have much choice."

With a few minutes to spare, we rejoined the dancers. I stood off to one side of the room, observing the others. One was smoking pot, another was drinking what looked like whisky on the rocks, and I don't care to know what the pills were that I saw one dancer pop into her mouth and wash down with a beer.

Candy leaned toward me. "As I said, stay away from drugs and alcohol, and you will be fine."

I nodded.

Benny stuck his head into the room. "Showtime, girls."

I followed Candy to the stage. She pointed to my assigned pole. I grasped it with my sweaty left hand, my heart pounded in my chest, and I had the sudden urge to use the bathroom to pee. I kept my back toward the audience. My strategy was to begin dancing without looking at the men and turn toward them once I was comfortable and gained my confidence.

## A VICTIM OF DESPERATION

The music started, the curtain opened, and Benny introduced each dancer. My hips began to sway to the music as I waited for my introduction.

"And tonight, in her debut, is the beautiful knockout, Jessica. Gentleman, let's make her feel welcome and show her your appreciation, monetarily, of course."

I twirled to the other side of the pole and did my best to ignore those sitting at the front tables. The blinding bright lights made it difficult to see the remainder of the room. In a way, I was thankful. I blocked out the judgmental stares caressing my body as I danced. I became a recluse, withdrawing into my own little space around the pole and danced. Benny's music choice made it easy to keep beat with the song. I often glanced at Candy. She was amazing. Her moves graceful, flexible, and alluring. I danced, knowing I was pale in comparison, but I danced.

Benny turned down the music. "That about does it for these gals. They have been working hard for your entertainment, so guys, let's show them your appreciation."

I followed Candy's lead as she went to the basket before her on the stage, collected her generous tips, and blew the crowd a kiss. I did the same. With my hands full of dollar bills, I followed her back to the dressing room.

"Looks like you did fairly well." Candy glanced at the wad of money in my hands before unlocking a drawer in her dressing table and put her cash in a zipped bank bag. "Here, you can put your cash in this one and keep it safely locked in my drawer until we leave for the evening." She handed me an empty bank bag.

I was tempted to count my money before putting it into the bag, but I did not want to appear too excited or greedy. I had never held so much money in my hands at one time.

Candy, Samantha, and I rested while the other three girls danced.

"Jessica, you danced well. I think the guys liked you." Samantha looked at me via my reflection in her mirror as she sat before her dressing table and brushed her long blonde hair.

"Thanks. I must admit, I was quite nervous, but I think I did all right for my first time."

"You did great." Candy smiled.

I danced the nine and eleven o'clock shifts, received even more tips for each than my first shift, and stuffed the dollar bills into my bank bag once I got back to the dressing room. I tried to relax during the next hour while toying with the idea of dancing the next shift, fully aware I would be dancing topless. I tried to justify my need for money while sacrificing my modesty. What would Heather think of what I was doing if she ever found out one day? Would she recognize the struggle I endured as a single mother, of doing what I had to do to provide for the two of us, or would she be ashamed of me?

Candy took a sip from her can of diet soda. "Wow, Jess, you are deep in thought."

Pulled from my thoughts, I looked at her and grinned, guilty of being caught.

"What are you thinking about?" She pressed.

"I was trying to decide if I am going to dance next hour." I grinned, ignoring the rising heat in my cheeks.

"And what did you decide?" Samantha's monotone question conveying my decision should be an easy one to make. She was busy adding blush to her cheeks before returning to the stage.

I sighed. "I'm going to dance. I need the money."

"You will be fine. Just pretend you are taking a shower at home." Candy smiled.

We took to the stage. If I thought I was nervous for my first shift, that paled compared to how nervous I was now. Even though I had put on deodorant before coming to work, my armpits were nearly dripping with sweat. My heart raced as I grabbed the pole with my back, facing the crowd. The music began, and I began to dance.

It was not long before Benny made the announcement, "It's time to take those tops off, ladies."

I turned away from the audience and continued to sway my hips to the beat of the music. The clasp of my bra was conveniently located between my breasts. I unhooked it and eased each strap over my shoulders one at a time. I thought the suspense would be more alluring. I slipped each arm free of the garment and tossed it aside before turning toward the pole and continuing to dance. What did it matter? I did not know any of these men. At least, I hoped I did not. As expected, the whistling, howling, and lude comments began, and the tips stacked like a small mountain in my basket.

At the end of my last shift, I was tired but excited. I had difficulty stuffing the money in my bank bag and zipping it shut.

"So, how was your first night?" Candy removed one of her false eyelashes while sitting at her dressing table.

"Easier than I thought." I pulled a clip from my hair.

## A VICTIM OF DESPERATION

"So, are you going to continue dancing?" She pulled off the second eyelash and placed it in the case with the first for safekeeping.

"Yes, for now. At least until I can get back on my feet financially." I removed another clip as I heard the echo of Benny announcing the close of the bar.

"Good. We can leave once we get changed."

I grabbed my clothes from her dressing table and changed in the bathroom. With my pink outfit in hand, I emerged and looked at Candy. "Is there a laundry service to do these?"

"No, take your outfit home and handwash it tonight so that it will dry in time for you to wear it tomorrow, or you may want to choose another outfit from the rack." She handed me a plastic bag to put it in.

As Candy drove me home, I reached into my bank bag and counted out the money I owed her. I held it out for her to accept as she parked the car in the apartment parking lot.

"Candy, thank you so much. Even though this was something out of the ordinary for me to do, I am very thankful for the opportunity you have given me."

She pushed my hand aside, unwilling to accept my repayment. "Sweetie, this one is on me. I just want you to get back on your feet."

Entering the building together, we parted ways, with her going down a set of stairs to the first floor and me ascending to the second floor. I nearly ran down the hall, fumbled with my keys in my haste, and pushed the door open with gusto. Locking the door once it closed, I emptied my bank bag onto the table and counted the money I had earned for the evening. Tears welled in my eyes as I stacked the bills into piles of one hundred dollars. I would be able to catch up on my unpaid bills quickly. Once I was in the black, I could buy a new couch to replace the hand-me-down I was using. Perhaps I could start looking for a new car, too, even buy Heather some clothes, and afford to shop at a real grocery store.

I tucked the money into my sock drawer, showered, and climbed into bed. Too excited to sleep. I reached over and set my alarm clock to pick up Heather in the morning. We could celebrate my good fortune by going out to eat breakfast, something I had never been able to do with her.

~

I started dancing every Friday and Saturday night and on occasion, Thursdays too. If it was a slow night, and I had driven to work, I could leave early. Heather spent every other weekend with Jim. Always

# A VICTIM OF DESPERATION

the absent father, at least her grandparents got to enjoy her company.

# Making Headway

It could hardly believe the amount of money I made dancing only two nights a week in the first month. I always paid myself first before paying my bills, and my savings account was growing substantially. My bills were paid in full. I had yet to shop for a new car or sofa but planned to do so soon. I would have to get loans for both and make payments. Unfortunately, I did not have any credit to qualify. I liked working only a few nights a week and spending my time off with Heather. My search for a new job and its prospects had drawbacks; childcare expenses, the distance away from home, and less pay than dancing.

## A VICTIM OF DESPERATION

I had just sat down for dinner with Heather when my phone rang. I went to the kitchen, picked up the receiver, and pulled the long phone cord toward me as I resumed my seat at the kitchen table.

"Hello."

"Hello, Jess."

I groaned inwardly. It was Danny. "Hi."

"What have you been doing since we broke up?"

"Well, I moved to a different apartment building, one I could afford by myself."

"You asked me to leave."

"Because you were cheating on me."

"A big mistake. I'm sorry."

I was in no mood for his apology. "So, what do you want?"

"I heard you were doing pretty good for yourself."

"You heard?" I clenched my teeth. Was he spying on me? "Who did you hear this from?"

"A friend told me he saw you dancing, and you are making lots of money."

"That's none of your business. I'm surviving the best way I know how and taking care of myself and Heather."

"That's good. I'm glad for you."

"So, what do you want?"

He sighed. "I want us to get back together."

I thought of his affair, how he preferred to go to the bars to hang out with his buddies instead of spending time with me, and his lack of maturity. It was as if he was stuck in time, forever an irresponsible teenager. Was he attempting to latch onto me because he had heard I was making lots of money?

"Sorry, it's not what I want. I have moved on." I stood and walked to the kitchen. "I wish you the best of luck." I hung up the phone.

I sat in my chair, only to have the phone ring again. I stomped to the kitchen and lifted the receiver. "What!"

"Woah, having a bad day, Jess?"

I exhaled. "Sorry, Mom. No, just a bad conversation with my ex-boyfriend. What's up?"

"I thought I would offer you a job."

My eyebrows raised, taken back by her offer. "A job?"

"Yes, I talked to your dad. He said you were making good money but needed employment that was a little more respectable."

I laughed. "Yes, exotic dancing isn't exactly a stellar skill and won't look good on a resume when applying for a job. However, I am making lots of money and working my way out of debt."

"Well, we have an opening at the mortgage company. Would you be interested?"

"What's involved?"

"Training and then you will be doing cold calls, which means you will have to seek out clients. It pays a commission, so it may take you a few months to begin earning an income. You can continue to dance until you earn a steady paycheck."

"I can give it a try. I'll have to make sure Aunt Angela can watch Heather."

"Sounds good. You will have to study for a test and get certified. I believe you can do most of it at home when you have time, but the sooner you test and pass, the sooner you can begin obtaining clients. Stop by my office to pick up the material."

"Ok. I will be there tomorrow."

Accepting the new opportunity, my life became a little more complicated. When I was not dancing evenings, I studied or at least tried to while caring for Heather. When she was down for the night, my studying was accompanied by the music emanating from the apartment below.

With Heather down for a nap one afternoon, I decided to wash a load of clothes and carried my heaping laundry basket to the laundry room down the hall. As I went to turn the knob on the door, it was pulled open by a rather nice-looking guy. He took a step backward and motioned for me to come into the tiny room.

"Thank you." I entered.

"You're welcome. I have something in the dryer, but the washer is free. Hey, if you aren't doing anything tonight, we're having a party on the first floor. Stop on by."

"Oh, you must live directly below me. I met a few of your roommates on the day I moved in. I get to listen to your music often."

"Sorry, they like to crank it up during a party."

I opened the lid to the washer and began putting in my clothes. "Well, I have to work tonight, but perhaps another time."

"Sure, stop by anytime you hear the music."

I dropped off Heather at my aunt's house before going to the dance club. I chose a cute royal blue sequence bra and thong bottom to wear for the night. I decided to put my hair into a high ponytail to whirl it about while I danced. My shifts remained the same as they did the first night I danced. At the eleven o'clock shift, a group of college frat guys sat in front of me. They hooted and hollered as I was introduced.

I had become more comfortable with dancing over the past few months and grown accustomed to the men staring with a menacing grin on their face as they fantasized. Others liked to talk, ask me out on a date, and shout rude compliments. I blamed the alcohol for their immoral behavior.

As I began to dance, I noticed one of the men in the group sat forward in his seat. He stared silently, watching every move I made. His face appeared kind and cute. He seemed out of place, uncomfortable in the club.

"OK, ladies, take a break." Benny lowered the music indicating my shift was over. I went to my basket.

"Hey, can I take you out for breakfast after you are done dancing tonight?"

I looked up and stared into the eyes of the man with the kind face. He smiled. There was a restaurant a block from the club. More than likely, this guy just wanted to have sex with me.

"No, sorry."

He reached into his pocket and emptied his wallet into my basket. "Seriously, I just gave you all of my money. I want to take you out for breakfast."

I smiled as I paused in gathering my money. "If you just gave me all of your money, how are you going to pay for breakfast?"

He turned in his chair, backhanded the guy in the chest next to him, and asked for some money. He turned back toward me and waved forty dollars in my face. "Now, will you go and have breakfast with me."

"No, sorry. I don't date customers." I gathered all my tips and rose.

"I'll wait here all night until you say yes."

"Good night, sir." I went to the dressing room.

I stuffed my money into my bank bag, and Candy locked it in her drawer. I plopped onto the vacant seat next to her. "There's this guy out there who has offered to take me out for breakfast."

"I guess he could offer you worse." Samantha laughed.

"He gave me all of his money and then had to borrow money from a buddy so he could take me out to eat."

"Oh, hell, he can buy me breakfast. I'm starving." Candy chimed in.

"Me too." Samantha joked.

I laughed.

When I went on stage for my next shift, Mr. Kind Face was sitting in the chair nearest to my pole. I scanned the table where he sat. His buddies had left. He held out his arms, palm up with the forty dollars waving in one hand, as if silently saying, "I'm still here and waiting." I shook my head in disbelief as I began to dance. He watched as I danced, loyally attentive and staring throughout my shift.

I collected my money when finished, and he leaned forward.

"I have waited all night. My friends even left me here. Please have breakfast with me."

This guy was relentless. "No, I don't date customers."

"It's not a date. It's just breakfast."

I sighed. I thought of Candy and Samantha. "If you are still here after I change my clothes, I will have breakfast with you, but you have to take my two friends too."

He smiled. "It's a deal."

"We will meet you by the door."

As promised, he was waiting for the three of us when we emerged from the dressing room. The four of us drove our cars to the restaurant and sat in a corner booth. Samantha and Candy sat next to each other, leaving my breakfast date sitting at the opposite end of the table from me.

"Hello, ladies. I'm glad you agreed to join me for breakfast. I'm Mike." He looked at me, waiting for me to say my name. Maybe he thought I had used a stage name.

"I'm Jessica, Jess."

"Samantha, but you can call me Sam."

"Candy."

The waitress brought menus and took our drink orders.

"So, tell us about yourself, Mike." Candy pried.

"I'm a student at the tech college. I major in engineering and captain of my soccer team."

"Do you go to exotic dance bars often?" Samantha tilted her head to one side.

"No, a group of my friends from the fraternity did it as a challenge. We were trying to see how many we could attend in one night."

"Yet you stayed behind when your friends left?" Candy continued the interrogation.

"Yes, I wanted to take Jess out for breakfast, and I'm happy the two of you decided to join us.

He conversed easily, was polite, and possessed the darkest blue eyes I had ever seen. He was tall, well built, and, I had to admit, quite good looking.

Overall, our breakfast was pleasant with engaging conversation. Mike was a senior at the tech college, two years older than me, received an out of state soccer scholarship, and was the team captain.

He walked each of us to our cars, with me being the last.

"I enjoyed having breakfast with you, Jess." He waited as I inserted my key into the lock on my van.

"It was nice eating with you as well. Thank you, Mike." I opened my door.

"So, can I have your phone number? I would like to do this again."

"Sorry, I don't date customers." I sat in the driver's seat. "It was nice meeting you. Thanks again for breakfast."

"Good night." Mike shut my door and stood next to my van like a sad puppy. I turned the key in the ignition and backed out of the parking spot. I returned his wave as I drove away, assuming our paths would never cross again.

The following week I took the test to sell mortgages and earned my certification. I began working in the office a few days a week, making cold calls. As forewarned, it was difficult to convince anyone to obtain a mortgage. It would be a while before I received any commission.

As I took to the stage Friday night, some of the regulars were seated in the front. I saw wedding rings on several of their hands. Why weren't they home with their wives or taking them out for dinner and a movie instead of ogling at other women and being frivolous with their money?

As I began my last shift of the night, a familiar face sat in a chair near the stage. Mike waved a twenty in his hand and mouthed the word 'breakfast.' I just smiled and nodded as I continued to dance.

It became his habit to show up for my last shift on Friday and Saturday nights and buy me breakfast. Inevitably the question arose.

"We have to stop meeting like this. How about we go on a date? I'll pick you up at your place, and we can go out."

I smiled as I paused with a slice of buttered toast in my hand. "I don't date customers."

"I like the sound of the title 'boyfriend.' If you bestow it upon me, then I wouldn't be your 'customer' anymore." Mike emphasized each word with quotation marks he made with his fingers in the air and displayed a cheesy smile after pleading his case.

I tilted my head to one side. I could not stop myself from grinning. "You have an answer for everything."

He scowled, then grinned. "No, more like creative solutions."

I laughed. This was getting serious. The one thing I had going for me was that Mike did not know where I lived. "I don't know if I have time for a boyfriend. I am busy raising my daughter and working two jobs."

## A VICTIM OF DESPERATION

He sat back in his seat. "Well, until I can change your mind, I will settle for having breakfast with you twice a week." He lifted his glass of orange juice, raised it, and with a nod of his head toasted in my honor before taking a drink.

The following Thursday, I put Heather down for the night, and I was trying to watch a program on TV, but the bass from the stereo below made it impossible to hear the show. I refrained from turning up the volume in fear of waking Heather and called Candy instead.

"Can you watch Heather while I go and talk to the guys below my apartment? They are having a party, and I need to convince them to turn down their stereo."

When she arrived, I explained Heather was sleeping, and I would return within a few minutes.

I descended the stairs and stepped into the chaotic noise of the first-floor hallway. The apartment door was open, so I took the liberty of entering.

"Hey, you finally came to one of our parties!" It was the guy who helped carry in my sofa.

I nodded. "Yes, it's kind of hard to watch TV when I can't hear it." I had to yell to be heard.

"Oh, the stereo too loud? Let me turn it down. I'm John. Here..." He turned toward the kitchen counter, grabbed a red solo cup topped with a foam of beer, and shoved it into my hand before leaving the room.

I looked at the kitchen corner and saw a keg of beer in a galvanized tub filled with ice. The volume of the stereo lowered to a tolerable decibel that no longer hurt my ears.

"Jess, glad you could come to the party."

The male voice from behind me sounded familiar. I turned to see Mike's tall, athletic physique standing in the doorway. From the grin on his face, he was happy to see me.

John returned. "Ah, I see you have met Mike. This little lady lives above us."

I camouflaged the unwanted advertisement of my residence with a grin.

"So, you live in this building." Mike looked at me as if a lightbulb turned on in his head.

"Yes, I'm afraid so."

"So, now that I know where you live, maybe I can stop by and take you out on a date."

I was being coerced, manipulated, yet flattered. I smiled. "Sure."

"I know you work tomorrow and Saturday, which I plan to take you out for breakfast both days. How about we go to the park on Sunday. We can bring your daughter, and she can play on the playground equipment."

## A VICTIM OF DESPERATION

It was my weekend to have Heather. "That sounds nice."

"What time should I pick you up?"

Heather usually took a nap after lunch. "Does three o'clock work for you?"

"Sure, we can grab a bucket of chicken for dinner."

It sounded like a lovely first date.

# As Luck Would Have It

Shortly after my nineteenth birthday, I received my first commission paycheck. With a substantial balance in my savings account and my bills paid in full, I was ready to purchase a new car. After visiting several dealerships and test-driving various vehicles, I decided on a car that seemed reasonably priced and fit my needs but could not qualify for the loan. I mentioned my dilemma to my mother when I reported for work the next day.

A few days later, my phone rang. I smiled, expecting to hear Mike's voice on the other end of the line.

"Hello."

# A VICTIM OF DESPERATION

"Hi, Jess."

I was surprised my mother's boyfriend was on the other end of the line. "Oh, hi. What's up?"

"Your mom said you found a new car that you like."

"Yes."

"But you can't qualify for a loan."

"That's what I was told."

"I have a way you can get a loan."

"Really?"

"Yes, I will co-sign the loan. You will be responsible for the payments, and the car will be in your name."

I didn't know what to think. I was overwhelmed. "Thank you. I appreciate your generosity."

We set a day and time to go to the dealership, file the paperwork, and purchase my new car. The clunky van was handed down to the next oldest member of my family.

Mike and I dated for a few months before moving into my apartment to finish out his senior year of college, and I continued to work two jobs. We went shopping for a new sofa and decided on an overstuffed, comfy one. Since I had established credit with the loan on my car, it was easy for me to apply for another loan and make payments. It was delivered the following week to my apartment, and I donated the old hand-me-down to charity.

My job at the mortgage company was finally paying off. I still danced at the club but reduced my hours.

After Mike graduated, he moved back home with his parents. We tried to date long-distance, which was reminiscent of when I dated Jim. We talked on the phone every day, but it was too hard. I had reached a breaking point.

I dialed his phone number.

"Hi, Jess."

"Hey."

"Oh, you sound serious."

"I am. This long-distance dating is getting too hard for me. Either we break up, or I move up there."

Mike had started a well-paying engineering job. Between the two of us, his income, and my savings, I was sure we could afford an apartment. He did not hesitate in replying.

"Then you will have to pack up your things and move up here with me. I will rent a two-bedroom apartment and come to help you move as soon as I secure our new home."

I smiled, relieved he had drawn the conclusion I had hoped for. "Sounds good. I need to tell my employers I am leaving. I think they would appreciate a two-week notice, so maybe by month's end, I will be there."

I began gathering boxes the next day, eager to start the next chapter in my life.

# Blessing And Prevention

Twenty years ago, I moved northward to a better life for myself and my daughter. I married Mike, the man who saw beyond the dancer I was on stage. He is a wonderful husband and a loving father to our children.

I smiled, realizing how blessed I am, how fulfilled my life has become.

Even though I was human trafficked, or labor trafficked, I guess you would call it, it could have led to something much worse, sex trafficking. I sometimes wonder if I was being groomed for it. Would they have kept me at the apartment forever, never to return home to my daughter, my family? I was lucky to get out of the predicament, and I often wonder what happened to Kendra, the others, and if they ever made it home. To this day, I do not know what my dad said to Josh, nor do I care to know. I am glad his plan was successful, and my leader drove me home. I am forever grateful for the kindness of Agnes, and yes, I still have her coat and shoes.

Some may wonder why I never went to the police to report what happened to me. Who would have believed me? I was young, I had gotten myself into the situation, and what would I have told them? After all, it was a job, and I agreed to go out of state. The term 'human trafficking' was nonexistent back then.

I released my white-knuckled grip on the steering wheel and took a deep breath to calm my rapidly beating heart as I stared at the sign, disgusted by its empty offer of entrapment. It sickened me to know that innocent, desperate, and unsuspecting young men and women may text the number and become victims of trafficking. My jaw tightened as I clenched my teeth.

"Not on my watch, you greedy assholes." I opened my car door, marched toward the sign, and yanked it from the ground. Opening my trunk, I tossed the deceptive advertisement inside and slammed the lid shut.

As I backed out of the parking lot, I vowed to destroy every sign I encountered, hoping to reduce the number of vulnerable people who may fall victim to the trafficker's nefarious way of life.

If you enjoyed reading

# A Victim Of Desperation,

please post your review on Amazon.

For more information about the author and her books, please visit www.BrendaHasseBooks.com

www.ingramcontent.com/pod-product-compliance
Lightning Source LLC
Chambersburg PA
CBHW031107080526
44587CB00011B/861